How to Be an Existentialist

By the Same Author:

How to Be a Philosopher
Sartre: A Guide for the Perplexed
Sartre and Fiction
The Sartre Dictionary

Also available from Continuum:

The Good, the True and the Beautiful, Michael Boylan
How to Make Good Decisions and Be Right All the Time, Iain King
How to Win Every Argument, Madsen Pirie
Sex and Philosophy, Edward Fullbrook and Kate Fullbrook

How to Be an Existentialist or How to Get Real, Get a Grip and Stop Making Excuses

Gary Cox

continuum

Continuum International Publishing Group

The Tower Building   80 Maiden Lane
11 York Road   Suite 704
London SE1 7NX   New York NY 10038

www.continuumbooks.com
www.garycoxphilosophy.com

First published 2009
Reprinted 2010 (twice)
First published in paperback 2011, 2012 (twice)

British Library Cataloguing-in-Publication Data
A catalogue record for this book is available from the British Library.

ISBN: HB: 978-1-4411-8843-4
        PB: 978-1-4411-3987-0

Library of Congress Cataloging-in-Publication Data
Cox, Gary, 1964-
How to be an existentialist, or, How to get real, get a grip,
and stop making excuses / Gary Cox.
    p. cm.
Includes bibliographical references (p.).
ISBN: 978-1-4411-8843-4
1. Existentialism. 2. Conduct of life. I. Title. II. Title: How to get real, get a grip, and stop
making excuses.

B819.C66 2009
142'.78–dc22

                                                                    2009005317

Typeset by Newgen Imaging Systems Pvt Ltd, Chennai, India
Printed and bound in the United States of America

Contents

Introduction

According to hard-line existentialists like Jean-Paul Sartre, whatever anyone does, ever, short of falling off a cliff, they *choose* to do it and are *responsible* for having done it. You, therefore, have chosen to pick up this book and open it. You are responsible for what you have done, even if you did so in the most idle and seemingly thoughtless way.

Perhaps you are killing time in a bookshop while you wait for your lover to arrive on the three o'clock train. You have no intention of buying this book because there are, after all, more important things to spend your money on than books. Your lover will expect you to treat them to a litre of designer coffee when that train gets in and Starbucks isn't cheap. Shortly, you will slip this book back on the shelf or the 3 for the price of 2 table display with that tiny grimace that says to anyone who might be spying on you, 'I *am* in here to buy a book, but *that* one isn't what I'm looking for.' Of course, I shouldn't assume your actions are so predictable. You have free will and will do as you choose. It is because you have free will, as everyone does, that you have the potential to become a true existentialist, if you're not one already that is.

Perhaps you are babysitting at a neighbour's house and having finally tucked their rug rat up in bed you have decided to check out their book collection to see how uncultured they are. This book has caught your eye because you know a lot or a little about existentialism, because it is a slim volume whereas most books on existentialism you've ever seen are fat and heavy, because it has a practical sounding title and not one that is totally obscure and pretentious like *Being and Time* or *Phenomenology of Perception*, because it appears to offer you the opportunity to become something quite mysterious and special, if only you can be bothered to read it all.

Perhaps you haven't picked this book up in an idle and thoughtless way at all, but with a very clear purpose. Good. With that kind of decisive attitude you are already well on your way to becoming a true existentialist. You ordered it on the internet the other day using that much abused credit card and found it lying below the letter box a moment ago. You've ripped open the bubble wrap lined envelope and dived straight in. You are looking for direction in your life and to that end you have decided to become an existentialist; to join that most peculiar and misunderstood of cults, that society which has no membership fee unless it is your sanity and your very soul, that exclusive club which is comprised of the kind of independent minded people who never join clubs or follow the crowd. The comedian Groucho Marx – not to be confused with the philosopher Karl Marx, although equally intelligent – once said, 'I don't want to belong to any club that will accept me as a member.' Well, a true existentialist wouldn't join a club that had members.

Once all the preliminaries are out of the way the first thing this book tries to do is explain in as simple and straightforward a way as possible what existentialism is. There are hundreds of other books that explain existentialism in far more philosophical detail, a few of which I have written myself, so if you want to get really deep into the theory of existentialism and possibly never surface again, check out the further reading section at the end of this book.

Having given it some thought, I've decided that a person can't be an existentialist unless he or she knows a bit about the philosophy or world-view of existentialism. Knowing a bit or even a lot about existentialism, however, will not, by itself, make you an existentialist. To be a true existentialist you also have to try to live in a certain way, or at least adopt a certain attitude to life, death and other people. Being an existentialist is definitely not just a matter of knowing stuff. For this reason, some of the most famous philosophers of existentialism were not in fact true existentialists at all, because although they knew a lot of theory they didn't live the life; they didn't practise what they preached.

Perhaps the main value of having a working knowledge of existentialism as a philosophical theory is that you will hopefully understand *why* it makes sense to live according to the existentialist world-view; why it is a more honest, more dignified, even a more moral way to live than other ways you might live.

The founders of Western philosophy, the Ancient Greeks, guys like Socrates, Plato and Aristotle, thought that the most important philosophical question in the universe, the question to which all other philosophical questions lead, is the question, 'How should I live?' If you are at all interested in becoming an existentialist then it is in fact the oldest and most important question in philosophy, 'How should I live?', that you are really interested in. Unlike a religion, existentialism does not say, do this, don't do that, eat this, don't eat that, follow all these petty rules and don't dare question them. Instead, it describes in a coherent, honest and uncompromising way what it is like to be a person passing through this weird and wild world. It aims to show you what you really are when all the nonsense and bullshit that is talked at you by scientists, preachers, parents and school teachers is binned. It aims to reveal to you that you are a *fundamentally free being* so that you can start living accordingly; so that you can start asserting your individual freedom, your true 'nature', rather than living as though you were a robot programmed by other people, social convention, religious dogma, morality, guilt and all the other age old forces of oppression.

Existentialism is all about freedom and personal *choice*. It is all about facing up to reality with honesty and courage and seeing things through to the end, as well as being about putting words like *choice* in italics. Becoming an existentialist requires a certain amount of effort. The real difficulty is keeping it up, sustaining it, maintaining what existentialists call *authenticity* while everyone, including yourself, and everything around you, wants you to give up like a big sissy and succumb to what existentialists call *bad faith*. Bad faith is a lot like what serious artists, musicians and rock stars call 'selling out'. Existentialists really hate, loathe and detest bad faith, but more about bad faith and authenticity later on. This book has a lot to say about authenticity and bad faith as they are at the heart of what existentialism and being an existentialist are all about.

I don't want to dwell too much on the effort required to be an existentialist because it is not in fact as hard as, say, fixing cars or learning a foreign language. Many existentialists, however, did learn to speak French or German long *before* they became existentialists. Being an existentialist isn't even exactly a skill. Or is it? To be honest I don't know. An existentialist – if I am one – always recognizes when he is not certain about something. He never tries to convince himself for the sake of his peace of mind that some half-baked doctrine is true. The Beatles once sang, 'You know I'd give you everything I've got for a little peace of mind.' Well, an existentialist wouldn't give you anything for a little peace of mind unless what he got in return was also true. An existentialist can stomach both uncertainty and hard truth. Or is that a philosopher? Never mind, an existentialist is a type of philosopher, just as existentialism is a branch of philosophy. You can make your own mind up at the end of this book whether or not you think being an existentialist is a skill.

Philosophers who have swallowed all the dictionaries in their university library, which is most philosophers, call existentialism *phenomenological ontology*, but I hope to avoid that kind of fancy jargon as much as possible in this lightweight and hopefully rather irresponsible book about responsibility and other such heavy matters. If you like fancy jargon, as far as more people do than will admit it, then read my other more serious books on existentialism, or more specifically, my books on the famous French existentialist, Jean-Paul Sartre. This is the second shameless plug for my other books in the space of this brief introduction, but then an existentialist – if I am one – should never be afraid of being too bold, or, for that matter, too withdrawn. Some existentialists, real and imagined, have extracted a lot of mileage out of the whole withdrawn, alienated thing.

So, if you've read this far and plan to read on, welcome to yet another self-help book that will change the way you think and feel about your life. Well, actually, the hope is that it will do more than that. The hope is that it will change the way you *behave*, the way you *act*. Existentialism holds that you can only truly change the way you think and feel about your life by *acting* differently, by acting rather than simply reacting, by asserting your will rather than simply allowing yourself to be swept along by circumstances, by always taking *responsibility* for yourself and what you do.

Existentialism, as said, is all about freedom. At the heart of freedom is choice and at the heart of choice is *action*. Action, then, is at the heart of existentialism, just as it is at the heart of human existence. 'To be is to do' says Sartre, summing up just how important he considers action to be. If people know only one thing about existentialism it tends to be the maxim, 'To be is to do.' The first I ever heard of Sartre and existentialism was when a friend told me this awful but accurate joke: 'To be is to do' – Jean-Paul Sartre. 'Do be do be do' – Frank Sinatra.

Finally, a disclaimer: If this book doesn't change the way you think, feel and act for the better, or in ways you hope and expect, then don't blame me! I am responsible for writing this book, but you are responsible for buying, borrowing or stealing it, for reading it, for what you make of it and for what you do or don't do in response to it. Blaming other people for things you are actually responsible for yourself is very fashionable. You could say we live in a *blame culture*, or more precisely, *a blame everyone but myself culture*. 'I did it because of the way I was raised.' 'I did it because I got in with the wrong crowd.' 'It's my teacher's fault I failed my exams even though I only turned up to half the lectures and bunked others early pretending I had a funeral.' 'It was McDonald's fault my coffee was hot and I burnt my mouth when

I drank it.' McDonald's are responsible for their coffee being hot, and for a lot of other things besides, but the customer is responsible for buying the coffee and drinking it. There are morbidly obese people waddling around out there who *chose* day after day to supersize themselves beneath the yellow arches who are now suing McDonald's for making them fat and unhealthy. Relinquishing responsibility and blaming others for what you do is very fashionable, but it was, is and always will be extremely unexistentialist, that is, extremely inauthentic.

Existentialism has often been accused of being a set of dangerous ideas. In 1948, for example, the Catholic Church in its infinite wisdom decided that Jean-Paul Sartre's atheistic, iconoclastic, anti-authoritarian, revolutionary existentialist ideas were so dangerous that they placed his entire works on the Vatican Index of Prohibited Books (the *Index Librorum Prohibitorum*), even those books he hadn't written yet! But really, there are no dangerous ideas, it is only what people *choose* to do with ideas that might prove dangerous, especially to the *status quo* and the powers that be, like governments and religions and other multinational corporations. Choose to do with these ideas as you please, or choose to do nothing – personally, I don't care – but remember what the existentialist philosophers say: to choose not to choose is still a choice for which you alone are responsible.

1 What is an Existentialist?

In *The Sartre Dictionary* I define the term *existentialist* as follows: 'Of or relating to the intellectual movement known as **existentialism**. A person, **Sartre** for example, whose work and ideas contribute to existentialism. Anyone who broadly subscribes to the theories and outlook of existentialism or attempts to live according to its principles.' In itself this definition doesn't tell us much. It is useful only in relation to the two cross-referenced entries indicated in bold type and the further cross-referenced entries indicated in those entries and so on. What is clear is that to fully understand what an existentialist is you need to understand what existentialism is. To that end I have written the longish chapter following this very short one, titled, not surprisingly 'What is Existentialism?'

What an existentialist is can't really be explained just like that all at once in a few words, in a short definition, hence the inevitable inadequacy of the definition given above. Instead, what an existentialist is and how a person becomes one are things that will emerge gradually during the course of this book. I am confident that by the end you will know what an existentialist is and what in broad terms it takes to become one. Accepting that the full meaning of *existentialist* is something that will emerge as we proceed, I'll begin by saying that to be a true existentialist a person has to fulfil three closely related critera:

1. A person has to know a reasonable amount about the philosophy and world-view of existentialism as worked out over many years by various thinkers such as Arthur Schopenhauer, Friedrich Nietzsche,

Jean-Paul Sartre, Simone de Beauvoir, Albert Camus, Samuel Beckett and Bugs Bunny.

Ok, so Bugs Bunny never helped to work out the theory of existentialism, but in accepting the reality of his situation, affirming his freedom and acting decisively on all occasions, Bugs has a truly authentic, existentialist-type attitude. He is certainly not a rabbit caught in the headlights of onrushing life. His sneering, anti-authoritarian, 'What's up Doc?', delivered while coolly crunching a stolen carrot, shows he is never taken by surprise and is ready for anything that life or Elmer Fudd can throw at him.

2. A person has to believe the philosophy and world-view of existentialism to some extent; hold that it is more or less correct. This does not mean they have to slavishly agree with everything existentialism claims as though it were some religious dogma. Short of rejecting it outright, they can be as critical of it as they like because if there is one thing that existentialism encourages it is questioning and the spirit of criticism. However, a person would not be an existentialist who knew about existentialism – having studied Camus or whoever – but rejected it all as total nonsense.

I dare to say that a person who has studied existentialism in any detail and has gained a reasonably sound understanding of it could not reject it as outright nonsense because it is so plainly not nonsense. Existentialism is a fiercely honest philosophy that confronts human life for what it really is, building its comprehensive, holistic thesis on the basis of certain undeniable facts or truths of the human condition, such as the truth that everyone is mortal, for example. As Charles Dickens once said, writing about an old lady's damning assessment of Mr Turveydrop, 'There was a fitness of things in the whole that carried conviction with it' (*Bleak House*, p. 227). Likewise, there is a fitness of things, a striking coherence of the various aspects of existentialism, that makes it a very convincing and plausible philosophy.

People who reject existentialism tend to do so not because they don't understand it but because they can't face it. As Nietzsche writes in *Beyond Good and Evil*: '"I do not like it." – Why? – "I am not up to it." – Has anyone ever answered like this?' (*Beyond Good and Evil*, 185, p. 107). As will be seen, understanding existentialism requires far more intellectual honesty and courage than cleverness and academic ability.

3. A person has to strive with some success to live and act in accordance with the findings and recommendations of existentialism. A person can know about existentialism and be convinced of its truth, but they are not a true existentialist if they make no effort to live the life.

It is quite possible for a person to know about existentialism, recognize the truth of it on an intellectual level, yet most or all of the time fail to live accordingly. To fail to live accordingly is to live in what existentialist philosophers call *bad faith*. Bad faith is a certain kind of bad attitude and I'll explain it in due course. For now, let it suffice to say that bad faith can be very difficult to avoid. We live in a human world built on bad faith. Bad faith offers convenient excuses, cop-outs and coping strategies, various distractions that seem to make everyday life more bearable.

So, the true existentialist knows about existentialism, believes in existentialism and continually strives to live according to existentialism. He or she continually strives to overcome bad faith and to achieve what existentialist philosophers call *authenticity*. Authenticity is the holy grail of existentialism, the great existentialist goal or ideal. More about authenticity later.

Interestingly, it seems it is quite possible for a person to be authentic without ever having heard of existentialism. Otherwise, we would be claiming that authenticity can only be achieved as the ultimate result of an intellectual exercise – as though you have to be able to read and study and have lots of time to swat to stand any chance of becoming authentic. Some people seem to hit on being authentic through their direct experience of life or because they choose to be particularly brave or genuinely philanthropic. Bugs Bunny is such a one, although who would be surprised to discover he reads Nietzsche when he is not busy exercising his will to power over Elma?

We might call such people, such admirable rabbits, true existentialists, but really they are not existentialists at all, they are simply what
academics who have studied existentialism describe as *authentic*. They
don't describe themselves as *authentic* because they don't think of
themselves in that way, they just get on with throwing themselves into
whatever they do without self-consciousness, misgivings or regret. It is
not actually at all authentic for a person to think he is authentic. The
person who declares 'I am authentic' thinks he *is* something, a fixed
entity, an authentic-*thing*. For reasons that will become clear, a person
who thinks like this or has this attitude is in fact in bad faith.

So, it is possible to be authentic without being an existentialist, but
it is not possible to be a true existentialist without striving hard to be
authentic. For the reader of this book who hopes to achieve authenticity, however, the key point is that the journey towards authenticity can
begin with learning about existentialism. Many people have been
inspired to pursue authenticity as a direct result of studying existentialism. Studying existentialism highlights the basic, inescapable, *existential* truths of the human condition, it exposes bad faith and emphasizes
the necessity of freedom and responsibility. Studying existentialism can,
therefore, be a process of profound personal enlightenment that influences the very nature of a person's way of existing in the world.

Philosophy is often seen simply as an ivory tower intellectual subject
with no bearing on real life, one of many subjects a person can do a
course in at college or university, and so the claim that profound personal enlightenment can result from the study of it sounds totally pretentious. For the Ancient founders of Western philosophy, however,
achieving enlightenment is the ultimate aim of studying philosophy. For
Plato, for example, the goal of studying philosophy is to gain knowledge of the highest truths. Armed with these truths a person has the
power to recognise the difference between reality and mere appearance. Plato firmly believes that the person who is truly able to distinguish reality from appearance will live accordingly, will cease to live
a lie. Like Platonism, although its view of reality is radically different,

existentialism also offers enlightenment and a way out of the deep, dark cave of ignorance, a way of seeing what is so rather than what only appears to be so.

2 What is Existentialism?

Brief overview and quick history lesson

It is interesting that thinking about what an existentialist is and how to be one has almost immediately taken us backwards to thinking about what existentialism is. That's how it is with philosophy. To go forwards you generally have to go backwards, especially to begin with. This is because when people start thinking about anything in any great depth they usually start halfway up some very shallow, very muddy conceptual shit creek; an obscure, overgrown place they've drifted into over the years as a result of making various assumptions they haven't thought through.

Philosophy is largely about dumping those assumptions overboard and backing carefully out of the shallow waters of the conceptual shit creek into the deep open ocean of the open mind. It is the done thing to mention the Ancient Greek philosopher Socrates at this point. Socrates said that philosophy is a peculiar practice because it builds by destroying and what it destroys is assumptions. Anyway, hopefully, from out there on the open ocean you will glimpse the mouth of the broad estuary that leads to the truth. The truth being, incidentally, that life is not a conceptual, but a very real, a very *existential*, shit creek! Well, there's no reason why the truth should be bright and shiny, whatever the poets say.

So, what is existentialism? Well, to put it simply, existentialism is a broad intellectual movement of largely continental philosophers, psychologists, novelists, dramatists, artists, musicians, film makers, comedians and assorted drop outs that developed in the nineteenth and twentieth centuries and remains influential today. Most existentialist philosophers are in fact French or German, with at least one Dane and a few Irishmen thrown in for good measure.

The British and Americans have always largely pooped the wild, totally happening existentialist party on the grounds that, in their opinion, existentialism is too broad and lacks philosophical rigour. They prefer to stay at home with their tobacco only pipes, their comfy slippers, a nice cup of tea and what they call *analytical philosophy*, which they like to hold up, not exactly in opposition to continental philosophizing, but as a more sensible, sober, straight-laced alternative. They like to bang on endlessly about logic and meaning in language – not that continental philosophers are indifferent to these things – while they contrive to say a great deal about as little as possible in the driest manner imaginable. To quote Nietzsche – always the most quotable philosopher – they definitely 'prefer a handful of "certainty" to a cartful of beautiful possibilities' (*Beyond Good and Evil*, 10, p. 40). They see continental philosophers, especially the most radical existentialist ones like Nietzsche and Sartre, as rather uncouth and grotesque with their big ideas about life, love, sex and death and their even bigger books.

Sartre once wrote a 2801 page book in three volumes called *The Family Idiot* and even at that length it wasn't finished! He intended to write a fourth volume but he went blind. Not from writing *The Family Idiot* but from blood pressure due to general over-indulgence. We only know *The Family Idiot* wasn't finished because Sartre told us. Obviously, nobody has actually read all the way to page 2801, except a very patient lady at The University of Chicago called Carol who translated the whole, vast unfinished monster into English.

The existentialist movement is defined by its shared concerns rather than by a set of common principles to which all existentialist thinkers subscribe, although there are principles common to many of them. Existentialism is primarily concerned with providing a coherent description of the human condition that fully recognizes and incorporates the fundamental or existential truths relating to that condition. In short, existentialism tells how it basically is for all of us in this tough, crazy world without bullshitting or pulling any punches. The fundamental or existential truths of the human condition according to existentialism are as follows:

None of us are fixed entities like chairs or stones, but indeterminate, ambiguous beings in constant process of becoming and change. We are all free and can't stop being free. We are all responsible for our actions and our lives are fraught with desire, guilt and anxiety, especially anxiety about our *being-for-others*. That is, our anxiety about what other people think of us. This leads us to suffer such irksome emotions as guilt, shame and embarrassment. And, if all this isn't bad enough, we are doomed to die from the moment we are born into a meaningless universe where God is at least very elusive and at most downright non-existent.

Strange to say, despite heaping up this long, grim list, existentialism is ultimately a positive, optimistic, anti-nihilistic philosophy! I kid you not. So why?

Well, because it outlines how you can go on to live an honest and worthwhile life in spite of the fact that human existence is ultimately pointless and absurd. The general idea is that you can't create a genuinely honest and worthwhile life for yourself on the basis of a fairytale. You have to build your life on an understanding and acceptance of how things really are, otherwise you will always be fooling and deluding yourself as you hanker after impossibilities like complete happiness and total fulfilment. Ironically, existentialism is saying, if you want to be happy, or at least be happier, stop struggling to achieve complete happiness because that way only leads to disappointment.

Some of the most unhappy people in the world are those who hold firmly to the false belief that complete happiness is achievable, that there is such a state as 'happily ever after'. They are constantly hurt and frustrated that they never manage, for example, to transform their life into an endless summer afternoon in a rose filled cottage garden. Such a paradise is unachievable, not only because the price of cottages in the country is beyond most people's financial reach, but because summer afternoons in the real world always turn to evening, because roses have thorns and their flowers wilt and because more than a few days in even the most beautiful garden becomes utterly boring. Actually, my cat spends everyday of his life patrolling the garden, his garden, and never gets bored, but he is a cat not a human. Oh, to be a cat! But be careful, it is inauthentic to wish you were something else, especially when it is *impossible* to be what you wish to be. True existentialists never *wish* they were something else, they *will* it, they actively strive to change themselves.

Many people have the silly idea, gleaned from movies, adverts and glossy magazines, that life is *perfectible*. The idea that other people out there somewhere have achieved the perfect life. So, they feel dissatisfied with the life they have or even downright cheated out of the life they think they deserve but don't have, the life that no one has. They yearn for a life of perfect happiness that is impossible, while failing to take control of the life they do have and make it more rewarding through decisive, realistic action. Existentialists are nihilists because they recognize that life is ultimately absurd and full of terrible, inescapable truths. They are anti-nihilists because they recognize that life does in fact have a meaning: the meaning each person chooses to give his or her own existence. They recognize that each person is free to create themselves and make something worthwhile of themselves by striving against life's difficulties. Life, or rather death, will win in the end, but what matters is the striving, the overcoming, the journey.

In a philosophical essay he wrote called *The Myth of Sisyphus*, the existentialist philosopher, Albert Camus, compares human existence to the plight of the mythical figure Sisyphus who is condemned forever to push a large boulder to the top of a hill only to watch it roll down again. Camus asks if life is worth living given that it is as absurd and ultimately futile as the plight of Sisyphus.

In choosing to live, in refusing the ever-present possibility of suicide, a person confers value and significance on a life that has no value or significance in itself. In choosing to live his life rather than end it a person takes on responsibility for his life. Camus' seemingly pessimistic account of the existential truths of the human condition yields an optimistic conclusion: although life's struggle has no ultimate purpose and always the same final result, a person can still create a sense of purpose through the struggle itself and through the way he plays life's game. If you think this is not a very optimistic conclusion then it is up to you to come up with a more optimistic conclusion that isn't based on false assumptions about the way life really is, a conclusion that isn't just a naïve fairytale or a wish list when you get to the bottom of it.

It was the Danish maverick Christian philosopher Søren Kierkegaard and the atheist and romantic philosophers, Arthur Schopenhaur and Friedrich Nietzsche, who, in their different ways, set the agenda for what later became known as existentialism. All of them were concerned with what we have been calling 'the truths of the human condition'. The concerns of Kierkegaard, Schopenhaur and Nietzsche were taken up during the first half of the twentieth century by Karl Jaspers (pronounced Yaspers), who coined the phrase 'existence philosophy', and by Martin Heidegger, Jean-Paul Sartre, Simone de Beauvoir, Maurice Merleau-Ponty and Albert Camus (pronounced Camoo). The last four in this list all knew each other and hung out together in bohemian Parisian cafés drinking cheap wine and smoking Gauloises. Heidegger didn't hang out with any of them. They would have shunned him if he'd tried to, not because he was older and German but because, unfortunately, he was a bit of a Nazi. This is an embarrassing fact that always has to be dealt with first whenever Heidegger's name comes up. To be precise, he was a one-time member of the German National

Socialist Party although he left in 1934. His national socialism is always hard to accommodate with the fact that he wrote *Being and Time*, one of the great texts of existentialism. Text as in book, that is, rather than a text you peck out on your mobile phone. Texting *Being and Time*, now that would be an achievement.

The writings of Heidegger, Sartre and the rest established existentialism as a distinct branch of philosophy. The ideas of these philosophers converge to form a largely coherent system of thought. At the heart of their system is the wonderful maxim 'existence precedes essence'. This maxim is generally attributed to Sartre who certainly uses it in a short book he wrote in 1946 called *Existentialism and Humanism*. It encapsulates a view fundamentally opposed to idealism that there are no ideal, otherworldly, God-given, abstract, metaphysical essences giving reality or meaning to particular things. There are particular things, like chairs and stones, and there is nothing beyond the series of particular things other than consciousness, which is nothing but consciousness *of* particular things. More on the *nothingness* of consciousness later.

With specific regard to people, 'existence precedes essence' refers to the view that each person exists first, without meaning or purpose, and strives thereafter to give himself meaning and purpose. A person's essence is to have no essence other than the one he must continually invent for himself. As Sartre's part-time girlfriend and long-time intellectual sparing partner, Simone de Beauvoir, often said, 'Man's nature is to have no nature.'

Now, before anyone gets on their feminist high horse, *man* here means men *and* women and is not singling out men. It is not gender specific. People who object to the use of the term *man* in this kind of context show their essential ignorance and petty mindedness. Back in the days when sociology and the other social sciences were busy inventing political correctness I had a very tedious argument with a very politically correct sociologist about the use of the terms *man* and *mankind*. I was keen to discuss with him some ideas I had about

Marxism before I taught them to the students we shared, but our conversation got stuck on the use of the word *man* and never went any further.

Anyway, it was Simone de Beauvoir herself who said, 'Man's nature is to have no nature,' and she practically invented feminism, even if she did allow Sartre to slap her around a bit! Actually, it's totally untrue that Sartre slapped de Beauvoir around. He wasn't big enough for a start. I just momentarily gave way to a sudden urge to jump on the creaking, overloaded, highly lucrative bandwagon of poorly researched, sensationalist biographies about Sartre and de Beauvoir; biographies claiming that at best they bit the heads of chickens for kicks and at worst were Nazi collaborators.

Mainstream existentialism, then, is anti-idealist, anti-metaphysical and atheistic. It sees mankind as occupying an indifferent universe that is meaningless to the point of absurdity. Any meaning that is to be found in this world must be established by each person from within the sphere of his own individual existence. A person who supposes that his meaning comes ready-made or that there is an ultimate purpose to human existence established externally by a deity or deities is deluded and a coward in face of reality. In short, he is an ignorant dork who needs to grow up and get real.

As indicated, not all thinkers who deserve existentialist credentials will endorse all of these viewpoints. The brilliant Russian novelist, Fyodor Dostoevsky, for example, clearly an existentialist thinker in many respects, is evidently, like the great Dane Kierkegaard, not an atheist. Existentialism is a broad church (though not a wide Gothic building) that includes religious thinkers like Paul Tillich, Martin Buber, Karl Barth and Gabriel Marcel and atheist thinkers like the novelist and playwright Samuel Beckett. I've spared you the pronunciations of the names of this lot as I'm not sure I know how to pronounce them all myself. Anyway, with the notable exception of Beckett, they are a pretty obscure bunch outside of equally obscure university Theology departments so you don't need to worry about them.

Bernardo Bertolucci, the Italian director who had Marlon Brando do unspeakable things with butter in *Last Tango in Paris*, explores many existentialist themes in his films, while the psychiatrist R. D. Laing defines the mental conditions of psychosis and schizophrenia in existentialist terms. Laing wrote a brilliant book about schizophrenia and psychosis called *The Divided Self: An Existential Study in Sanity and Madness*. I'm in two minds about recommending it to you as by the time you've finished reading it you'll be worrying you've got all the symptoms. I did and so did I! Laing appears to have written *The Divided Self* partly as a way of generating more clients. Shakespeare, particularly the mature Shakespeare of the great tragedies like *Hamlet* and *King Lear* and all that really heavy stuff, is profoundly existentialist. Maybe it was even Shakespeare who invented existentialism. Existentialism, as a way of viewing the human condition, this mortal coil, has been around a lot longer than the term itself. Sartre, probably the most famous existentialist of all, initially rejected the term, preferring 'philosophy of existence' or that old mouthful *phenomenological ontology*, but never shy of a bit of self-promotion Sartre soon adopted it in face of popular insistence on it.

I said in my introduction that being an existentialist requires a certain amount of effort. Becoming an existentialist is not for the weak-minded or the faint-hearted, for people who give up at the first hurdle. By reading this far you have proved you are not the sort of person who gives up at the first hurdle. You have certainly cleared a few hurdles to get to here. So, well done and all that. If you find such praise patronizing, as many would-be existentialists will, I'll say, 'Get your arse in gear soldier, we've still got miles to yomp to the end of the trail with our eighty-pound loads.' As the British Royal Marines and Parachute Regiment say, 'Remember the long march across The Falklands.' Not being weak-minded or faint-hearted you won't be phased when I tell you that so far this chapter has only provided an overview of existentialism; the background to it and a short history lesson in it. We need to dig down deeper to where the ground gets that much harder in order to discover why existentialism makes the claims it makes and what these claims really mean. Why, for example, does Simone de Beauvoir claim that man's nature is to have no nature, and what does it mean to say consciousness is nothing in itself?

Despite what its harshest critics say, none of whom understand it properly anyway, existentialism is a largely coherent theory of the human condition rooted in the best traditions of Western philosophy. It is really all based on a theory of the nature of human consciousness the origins of which can be traced back to the brilliant German philosopher, Immanuel Kant, and his equally brilliant, equally German successor, George Wilhelm Friedrich Hegel. Existentialism is in fact only a branch or a development of a philosophical theory called *phenomenology* which can certainly be traced back to Hegel and to some extent Kant as well. No philosopher operates in a vacuum and every philosopher owes something to his predecessors. So, when looking for the source of phenomenology it is not possible to implicate Hegel without implicating Kant. And a big influence on Kant was the Scottish philosopher David Hume, and so it goes back into the mists of time. It is certainly possible to identify phenomenological type ideas in Hume.

Anyway, it is the phenomenological theory of consciousness that underpins all the other claims that existentialism makes about time, freedom, personal relations, bad faith, authenticity and so on. Not surprisingly then, it is this theory of consciousness that we must look at. It is a wonderful, profound theory full of initially absurd sounding paradoxes that get more obviously true the more you think about them. Above all, it is the key to understanding existentialism. In a sense, it *is* existentialism. Tell that to the next person who asks you what existentialism is: 'Existentialism is a theory of consciousness.'

Actually, there are lots of things that existentialism is. Some people may know the 'Love is . . .' cartoons, posters, badges and T-shirts founded in the sixties by Kim and still going strong. 'Love is sharing your gloves.' 'Love is the demand to be loved.' In fact, the second one is Sartre's. He wrote it in 1943. So maybe he influenced Kim's famous cartoon series. Existentialism is a bit like 'Love is . . .'. Quite a few formulations would neatly complete a sentence beginning 'Existentialism is. . . .': 'Existentialism is a theory of the human condition.' 'Existentialism is not for the faint hearted.' 'Existentialism is heavy stuff.' 'Existentialism is not that heavy really.'

Existentialism and consciousness

The mind, or what most existentialist philosophers prefer to call *consciousness*, is not a thing. In fact, it is *nothing*, or to be more precise, it is nothing in itself. This is a startling claim and is likely to sound ridiculous at first, but stay with the idea as it makes perfect sense when you get used to it. Sartre was so convinced that consciousness is nothing in itself that he called his greatest book on existentialism, *Being and Nothingness* – the nothingness referred to in the title being consciousness. Actually, to be precise, he called his greatest book, *L'Etre et le néant*, which translates more accurately as *Being and Non-being* but *Being and Nothingness* is now so well established as the work's enigmatic sounding English title that it is unlikely any publisher would ever dare mess with it.

In trying to make sense of the claim that consciousness is nothing, a nothingness or a non-being, you have to begin by accepting that not everything that comprises this amazing universe of ours is made of stuff, matter, atoms or whatever it is material things are made of deep down at the tiniest level. For example, is time a thing? I can measure time with a clock and even, as we say, feel it passing quickly or slowly, but I can't grasp a handful of it or stick a pin in it. It is real enough but it is not a thing. The same can be said for what are commonly called *states of mind*, like belief, expectation or anxiety.

Numbers too play a huge part in our lives but they are not material, or what philosophers call *corporeal*. A child can hold a bright green plastic number 3 in his hand but he is not holding three itself; three itself is not green and plastic. Surely, that green plastic thing in his little hand is only a symbol of the abstract idea or concept of three, a thought that is the same for all thinking creatures anywhere in the universe whether they symbolize three as *trois*, *3* or ☺☺☺. And the same can be said for other mathematical symbols, +, −, = and so on. The = sign does not indicate a *thing* called equivalence that you can hold in your hand, it indicates a *relationship* between two or more things . . .

That's as far as I'll go with the maths examples as I don't want to turn readers off who have an aversion to maths. You may be relieved to know that existentialism doesn't have a great deal to do with maths and you certainly don't need to be good at maths to become an existentialist. All I am doing with these maths examples is pointing out a whole vast area of reality – the world of maths – that isn't material.

Training shoes, tug boats and adhesive tape are material objects, whereas equivalence is a *relationship*. A philosopher was once asked what different kinds of entities are in the world. He replied, 'Things and relations'. Consciousness definitely falls into the second category. It is a relationship rather than a material thing. Another philosopher who was asked the same question replied, 'Things and chaps'. He was an ex boys private school type and probably didn't know many women, but his 'things and chaps' makes the all-important point that on the one hand the world contains objects and on the other hand subjects or consciousnesses.

Some scientific minded people who want to over-simplify the world and reduce everything to the behaviour of small physical particles will argue that consciousness is a brain state, that it is just millions of electro-chemical reactions in the brain. Now, we have to tread a bit carefully here. In arguing that consciousness is nothing in itself, that it is a relationship rather than a thing, existentialists are not claiming that consciousness exists, or can exist, without the brain. Consciousness must be what existentialists call *embodied*. Rather boringly perhaps, they don't go in for the idea of free-floating consciousnesses, out of body experiences, ghosts and all the rest of it. Consciousness requires brain

and, as the evidence of life strongly suggests, if you destroy t
you destroy the consciousness.

However, this is not to say that consciousness is *just* brain activity;
that consciousness is *reducible* to brain activity. When you see a certain
area of neurons lit up and active on a brain scanner you are not seeing
a person's thoughts. All you know is that these neurons become active
when he thinks of cream cakes and desires them. And if you delved
into his brain you would not find his thoughts of distant mountains or
his expectation of travelling there soon, and certainly you would not
find a little picture of mountains inside his skull. All you would find, if
you could see anything at all with all that blood, is a folded lump of
greyish fat.

This is because his desires, his thoughts, his expectations – although
he can't have them without having a brain inside his head – are not
things inside his head! They are aspects of his *relationship* with the
world. His desire is not just x, y, z neuron firing pattern but desire of that
cream cake there on the plate in front of him. His thoughts are of
mountains. If I think of mountains I am not looking at a little picture of
mountains inside my brain with what is called my mind's eye, I am
thinking of and *intending* mountains out there in the world. If I have a
feeling of expectation with regard to the mountains it is because I am
expecting to go there. If expectation was just a chemical state of my
brain then I could feel expectant without actually expecting anything,
which is surely impossible. 'I expect my brother to arrive here in five
minutes even though I know he is on the other side of the world right
now!' It just doesn't make sense does it? A person feels expectant
because he has an expectation *of* something. So, desire is desire *of*
something, thoughts are thoughts *of* something, expectation is expectation *of* something and so on.

These are all ways of saying that consciousness is not reducible to
brain states, that it is nothing in itself, that it is primarily a *relationship*
to the world of which it is conscious. Phenomenologists – the broader
group of philosophers to which existentialists belong – sum all this up

with the maxim 'consciousness *is* consciousness of __'. In that big book, *Being and Nothingness*, which some people call the bible of existentialism, Sartre writes: 'To say that consciousness is consciousness of something means that for consciousness there is no being outside of that precise obligation to be a revealing intuition of something' (*Being and Nothingness*, p. 17). The view that consciousness is consciousness *of* __ is known as the theory of *intentionality*.

The theory of intentionality was first thought up by a German psychologist called Franz Brentano and developed by another German, Edmund Husserl. Phenomenology is like a Mediterranean hotel, lots of Germans, although these Germans spent their time up in their rooms writing rather than down by the pool hogging the sun-loungers with their big towels. Husserl was not exactly an existentialist but his ideas about consciousness had a huge influence on two of the biggest existentialists of all, Heidegger and Sartre. It is fair to say that Husserl was Sartre's biggest single influence. As a young man in 1933 Sartre went to Germany for several months to study the philosophy of Husserl, and in 1937 he even wrote a book called *The Transcendence of the Ego* dedicated to an analysis of Husserl's philosophy of mind. The theory of intentionality states that consciousness is *intentional*, it always *intends* something, it is always directed towards something, it is always *about* something. Some modern philosophers even refer to the intentionality of consciousness as the *aboutness* of consciousness. Just as a reflection in a mirror is nothing beyond what it reflects, nothing in itself, so consciousness is nothing beyond what it is about and directed towards.

The theory of intentionality implies that because consciousness is always of or about something and nothing beyond that, any attempt to investigate consciousness always leads immediately to an investigation of whatever consciousness is of or about. Phenomenologists, including existentialists, seek to understand consciousness by investigating the way in which different *phenomena*, different *intentional objects*, appear to consciousness. An intentional object is whatever consciousness is about, be it perceived, imagined, believed or felt.

Love, for example, is an intentional object, a collection of appearances to consciousness. David's love of Victoria does not exist as such, it is an intentional object (in this case an intentional psychic object) comprised of David's happiness when he sees Victoria, his feelings of desire when he thinks of her, the positive things he says about her, his wish or intention to help and protect Victoria and so on. These appearances are not manifestations of an underlying love in itself, they are the love. There is no love in itself beyond the various appearances that we collectively describe as David's love of Victoria.

A physical object is also an intentional object, a collection of *appearances* to consciousness. Far away, a pen, for example, appears small. Close up it appears large. When turned, different sides appear and disappear. Its shape appears differently as its orientation changes, its colour alters with the light. It makes a sound as it is thrown back on the desk. The same things can be said of the pen as was said for love. There is no pen in itself beyond the various shifting appearances that we collectively describe as this pen. So, according to Brentano and Husserl and their many phenomenologist followers, things are actually just collections of appearances. Things must be *reduced* to their appearances in order to be understood correctly.

The startling conclusion to be drawn from all this is that phenomena, all the different kinds of physical and non-physical things which comprise the world, are collections of appearances to *consciousness*.

It is worth noting Sartre's position on this. For his part, Sartre seems at times to want to resist the startling conclusion regarding appearances, arguing that although appearances appear to us, they exist as they appear to us independently of us. A mug, for example, is a collection of appearances to us, but it is also out there 'being a mug' quite independently of anyone looking at it, touching it, drinking from it. More often, however, he is less of a realist about appearances, insisting that appearances must appear to someone in order to have any reality as appearances. As he so clearly states right at the start of *Being and Nothingness*, 'Relative the phenomenon remains, for "to appear" supposes in essence somebody to whom to appear' (*Being and Nothingness*, p. 2). In short, mugs only exist as mugs when appearing to someone.

When Sartre argues like this he comes across as a so-called *transcendental idealist* in the style of the great German philosopher, Immanuel Kant. Kant is to philosophy what Rome is to geography, all roads lead to him sooner or later. In lots of places in his writings Sartre argues that when there is no consciousness present on the scene there is only what he calls *undifferentiated being*. This undifferentiated being just *is*, and that is really all that can be said about it. It has no properties, no features, no characteristics. It is even more bland than daytime TV. It doesn't even have a past or a future. Philosophers often argue about whether or not a falling tree makes a noise when there is nobody around to hear it. Well, if there is only undifferentiated being when there is no consciousness around then when there is no consciousness around there aren't even any individual trees to fall and make a noise. There is no individual anything!

Sartre argues that undifferentiated being is differentiated and divided up into distinct phenomena by consciousness. Consciousness, he says, is a nothingness or a negation that places particular negations, negativities, lacks and absences into undifferentiated being that, so to speak, carve it up into particular phenomena – this as distinct from that, this as not that, this as external to that, here as not there, then as not now and so on. In an excellent and much used book he wrote called *Using Sartre*, Professor Gregory McCulloch, a teacher of mine way back in the mists of time, summarizes Sartre's position as follows: 'Sartre seems committed to the view that the non-conscious world is, in itself, a "fullness" or "plenitude", an undifferentiated mass of porridge-like stuff which is moulded into the known world by us' (*Using Sartre*, p. 115). Fair point professor, but compared with Sartre's undifferentiated being, porridge is positively rich in properties . . . in appearances.

This is obviously radical if not complicated stuff but the key point to take away is that Sartre, like Kant, is saying that the world of phenomena we are aware of is a *synthesis* of whatever is 'out there' and the activity of consciousness upon whatever is 'out there'. We are not just passive observers of the world. The world we know is a product of the intimate *relationship* that exists between consciousness and being. In the words of the Ancient Greek philosopher Protagoras, 'Man is the measure of all things.'

You may be thinking that we seem to have drifted a long way from the high road into a lot of obscure, pointless, high-falutin' philosophical speculation. You may be starting to wonder what all this philosophical bobbing and weaving has to do with the main agenda of becoming an existentialist. Well, first, to be an existentialist, you need to know what existentialism is about, and this is exactly what it is about when it comes to the subject of consciousness. Most importantly though, in showing that we are not just passive observers of the world, that we are the measure of all things and so on, Sartre and the rest are showing us that the world, our world, is constantly subject to our active interpretation of it. We constantly encounter a world characterized and defined by the motives, intentions and attitudes we choose to have and the evaluations we choose to make. This is not to say that the world is anything we wish it to be, far from it, but it is to say that there is a very real sense in which the world for each person is a product of the attitude with which he or she approaches it. This realization is, or should be, enormously empowering. Personal empowerment is right at the top of the existentialist agenda.

There used to be a car advert on TV saying 'Confidence is everything', and it is the kind of cliché you see on work place motivational posters that are meant to inspire employees to shuffle more paper or produce more goods. You know, the kind that picture tug-o-war teams with the word 'TEAMWORK' or a salmon swimming up stream with the word 'PERSE-VERANCE' or George W. Bush with the words 'YOU DON'T HAVE TO BE TOP OF THE CLASS TO BE TOP OF THE HEAP'. The picture for 'CONFI-DENCE IS EVERYTHING' might well be a tightrope walker, as a tightrope walker must think positively and remain confident or he will fall off.

The person who chooses to be positive and confident or, at least, genuinely tries to be positive and confident, will encounter a very different world from the person who chooses to be negative and timid.

* * *

According to Sartre and other existentialist philosophers, *differentiated being*, the richly varied world of phenomena we all inhabit, is grounded or based on consciousness, or at least, upon the negations, lacks and absences that consciousness places into being. In other words, phenomena are not grounded or based on being but on particular lacks or privations of being. Particular privations of being occur when, for example, being is questioned. The relationship of consciousness to the world is very much characterized by a questioning attitude. This attitude is not just the capacity to judge that something is lacking but the constant expectation of a discovery of lack or non-being. If I look to see if my cake is baked, for example, it is because I consider it possible that it is *not* baked. Even supposing there are cakes apart from consciousness of them, a cake can only be 'not baked' for a consciousness that experiences the cake in the mode of not yet being what it will be in future. The cake does not lack being baked for itself, it lacks being baked for a consciousness that has desires and expectations regarding it.

The following example of an acorn and an oak tree helps to make clear what existentialists understand by lack: In itself an acorn lacks nothing, it is simply what it is. In order to understand it as a potential oak tree it must be judged in terms of the oak tree that is presently lacking. The *meaning* of the acorn is based on the non-being of the oak tree as that which the acorn presently lacks. The acorn itself does not lack the oak tree. The acorn lacks the oak tree only for a consciousness that is capable of projecting forward in time beyond the acorn towards the not-yet-being or non-being of the oak tree. It is the non-being of the oak tree that gives the acorn its meaning for consciousness. For consciousness the acorn exists in the manner of being the non-being of the oak tree. As a meaningful phenomenon, the acorn is understood as what it is by virtue of what it lacks.

Consciousness constantly introduces non-being, negation, negativities, lack, absence into the world in order to make sense of it and to act purposefully within it. In technical terms we can say, phenomena are grounded not upon being but upon non-being, they arise for consciousness when consciousness places particular negations into undifferentiated, porridge-like being so giving rise to differentiated being.

In more down-to-earth terms we can say, a situation is always understood not in terms of what it is but in terms of what it lacks for the person encountering it. In itself a situation is a fullness of being, it lacks nothing, but in itself it is precisely not a situation because to be a situation it must be a situation *for* someone, the situation *of* someone. The lacks that make it a situation, that give it future possibilities and so on, are given to it by the person for whom it is a situation.

A person interprets every situation according to his desires, hopes, expectations and intentions. Every situation a person encounters is understood as presently lacking something desired, expected, intended or anticipated. As said, the situation in itself does not lack anything; it lacks something only for the person whose situation it is. What a situation lacks is what I lack. If one of my car tyres is flat it is I, not the car itself, that lacks four good tyres. More to the point, it is *my purposes* that lack a functioning car.

Consciousness is always predisposed to find something lacking because lack is intrinsic to the very meaning of every situation for any particular consciousness. This is why, according to existentialist philosophers, a consciousness, a person, can never be completely satisfied. A person will always interpret a situation in terms of what it lacks for him. If he is cooking, his meal lacks being cooked. If he is eating, his meal lacks being eaten. If he is half way through a movie the movie lacks an ending so far. If the movie is poor and he does not care about the ending then his situation lacks interest. If he is tired he lacks sleep (tiredness is lack of sleep). If he has just awoken and is ready for the day he lacks the things he hopes to achieve that day and so on and so on.

In general, a person always lacks the future towards which he is constantly heading, the future which gives meaning to his present actions and beyond which he hopes in vain to be fulfilled and at one with himself. Ever onward, the endless march of time, towards a future that is presently lacking, an absent future that will fall into the past as soon as it is reached, a past with its own absent future. It seems that the endless march of time constantly cheats us of what we are, prevents us from becoming one with ourselves, but really, what we are *is* this endless march forward in time, creatures that can never become one with themselves.

Perhaps this is the harshest of all the existential truths of the human condition. You will always experience some lack, some boredom, some dissatisfaction. You will always be waiting for some current problem to become a thing of the past, you will always be looking for future fulfilment until death is the only fulfilment, the only possibility, left to you. This is not a bad thing, it is just the way it is, so you would be wrong to get depressed about it, although many people do. A true existentialist doesn't get depressed about it. He or she says, 'Ok, so that's the way it is. Never mind, I'm still going to make the most of my life, my relentless journey to nowhere, *my freedom*.'

Closely linked to the phenomenon of existential lack is the phenomenon of *existential absence*. Sartre – he often has the best examples – describes the experience of discovering that his friend Pierre is absent from the café where he has arranged to meet him (*Being and Nothingness*, pp. 33–35). 'When I enter this café to search for Pierre, there is formed a synthetic organisation of all the objects in the café, on the ground of which Pierre is given as about to appear' (*Being and Nothingness*, p. 33). Pierre, as the person Sartre expects to find, is existentially absent. This existential absence is distinct from an abstract and purely *formal absence* that is merely thought. 'Wellington is not in this café, Paul Valéry is no longer here, etc.' (*Being and Nothingness*, p. 34).

The distinction between existential and formal absence emphasizes that non-being does not arise simply through judgements made by consciousness after encountering the world, but that non-being belongs to the very nature of the world as it is for consciousness. Pierre's absence from the café, unlike Queen Victoria's, is not merely thought. His absence is an actual event at the café that characterizes the café as the place from which Pierre is absent. Think about this next time you are in Starbucks waiting for your friend to turn up. You might also want to dwell on why existentialists always seem to end up in cafés.

A person's entire world can exist in the mode of the negative; in the manner of not being the presence of whatever is desired. The misery of missing someone or something is rooted in this negating of the world. The misery of withdrawing psychologically from a drug, for example, lies not so much in the loss of the pleasure the drug gave, but in the reduction of the whole world to a dull background that has no other significance or value than to be the perpetual affirmation of the drug's absence. Nothing interests or inspires a withdrawing addict except their absent fix. Even things that have no direct association with their fix refer the addict to their fix simply because they are not their fix. The addict's entire world is reduced to not being heroin, alcohol, nicotine, coffee, chocolate, base jumping, on-line gambling or whatever their personal fix happens to be.

Temporality

Time or temporality has been lurking in the background of a lot of what has been said so far. It is useful to take a closer look at what phe-nomenologists and existentialists say about temporality, as in many ways a proper understanding of time and the so-called *temporality of consciousness* is the key to understanding the whole existentialist philosophy of life, the universe and everything.

When a person takes a deep breath and knuckles down to the challenge of reading Sartre's *Being and Nothingness* – the philosophical
equivalent of swimming the English Channel only more taxing on the
brain – he or she finds that the following paradox keeps cropping up in
various forms: *The being of consciousness is not to be what it is and to
be what it is not*. Sartre himself says, '. . . human reality is constituted
as a being which is what it is not and which is not what it is' (*Being and
Nothingness*, p. 86). Many people, including trained philosophers, are
so shocked and outraged by this paradox, this apparent excursion to
Loonyville, they throw the big book down with a thud and never go
near it again, never knowing all the wonderful insights they have
missed. Certainly, this paradox does appear absurd on the face of it, as
do all paradoxes. How on earth can something be what it is not and
not be what it is?

Well, we have already seen that consciousness is nothing in itself,
that it exists not as a thing but as a relationship to the world. So,
already we have entertained the idea of consciousness existing as a
relation to something that it isn't; of it being dependent for its bor-
rowed being on what it is not. However, the best way to fully grasp the
meaning and sense of the paradox of consciousness is to think of it in
terms of the ceaseless passage of time, something we are all very familiar with.

Consciousness is not just *in* time like an object getting older with
every day that passes, it is, as the existentialists say, *essentially temporalized*. This means that it is always its past which is no longer and its
future which is not yet. It is in constant temporal motion away from its
past towards its future, so much so that there is really no such moment
as the present. Consciousness does not hop from one present moment
to the next. The present for consciousness is only its *presence* to the
world as a being constantly flowing forward in time. Existentialists refer
to this constant temporal motion of consciousness as *temporal transcendence, temporal surpassing* or *temporal flight*. Consciousness constantly transcends, surpasses and flees what it is – what it *was* – towards

the future at which it aims. Here is Sartre's paradox of consciousness again with the temporal stuff added in and hopefully this time it makes a lot more sense: *The being of consciousness is not to be what it is (its past) and to be what it is not (its future)*. Sartre himself says, 'At present it is not what it is (past) and it is what it is not (future)' (*Being and Nothingness*, p. 146).

The three dimensions of time that we are all so familiar with – past, present and future – are not really separate. Each one only has reality or meaning in terms of the other two. What is now a person's past was once his future at which he aimed. On Friday the Saturday cycle ride I plan so carefully is *not-yet*. As I arrive home from it the event immediately becomes *no-longer*. Not-yet becomes no-longer so consistently that Sartre insists it is more accurate to refer to the past as a *past-future*. What is now my past was once my future. Similarly, what is in my future, if it comes to *pass*, will so undoubtedly become part of my past that it is more accurate to refer to my future as a *future-past*.

As for the present, we have already seen that it is not a fixed moment – there are no fixed moments for consciousness. The present is simply the presence of consciousness to the world as a being that constantly transcends the past towards the future. In other words, consciousness is never in the present, it is only ever present (has presence) as a being endlessly passing on towards the future. Like an object in motion consciousness is never *there* or *there*. To think that consciousness can ever be fixed in the moment is to suppose time can be frozen. Consciousness is constantly no longer where it was and not yet where it will be.

The really mind-blowing claim that phenomenologists and existentialist philosophers make about time is that there is no such thing as time apart from consciousness. It is consciousness that brings time into the world, consciousness that temporalizes the world. When a cup is broken there is as much stuff as there was before it was broken but the cup has gone. The broken fragments themselves do not recall that there *was* a cup, only consciousness can do that. The past cup exists only for consciousness; the fragments have a cup-like past only for consciousness. If something *was* something only for consciousness, then it is only for consciousness that anything has a past, only for consciousness that anything can be truly destroyed. Pretty much the same can be said for the future. A fire does not know its future is to burn down to a pile of ashes, only consciousness can know that the future of a blaze is a pile of ashes, which is the same as saying that the ash heap future of the fire exists only for consciousness.

Of course, to claim that there is no time apart from consciousness is not necessarily to claim that apart from consciousness there are no processes of becoming in the world; that without consciousness nothing comes into or goes out of existence, grows up or gets burnt down. It is simply to argue that apart from consciousness there is no awareness of the processes of becoming, growth, decay, destruction; no notion of a past or a future for any particular present.

Let's go back to that acorn again – it hasn't grown much since we last talked about it and it can still be identified as an acorn. As it is in itself apart from anyone being conscious of it, an acorn is in process of becoming an oak. Yet in doing so it is not *aiming* at becoming an oak. Unless I am very much mistaken and the kind of thing that happens in fairy tales is true, the young acorn is not down in the good earth saying to itself, 'Come on then little acorn, big effort, I've got to grow into a big tall oak tree just like my gnarled old mom.' It is not projecting itself towards any future goal and it has no *futurizing intention* whereby it recognizes itself as something that presently lacks itself as an oak tree. As becoming an oak is not a *project* for the acorn, and definitely not a conscious project, it is correct to say that the acorn has no future. It has a future only for a consciousness that understands that the acorn is not yet an oak tree but will be an oak tree in future.

If the claim that there is no time apart from consciousness is understood in this way then it ceases to be as crazy as it first sounds. Understood in this way, claiming that there is no time apart from consciousness is not equivalent to claiming that nothing happens apart from consciousness. Rather, it is equivalent to claiming that apart from consciousness the world as it is in itself is without the features of no-longer and not-yet.

All this talk about time describes how it is for each and every person to be in the world, the awkwardness of our inescapable human condition. Not least, it reveals why people always feel slightly dissatisfied, why they always feel that something is lacking. Something *is* always lacking, namely the future. The future never satisfies and fulfils us completely because we only fulfil our future intentions for them immediately to become part of our past, for them to become a past-future on the basis of which we must again launch ourselves towards a new future, towards a new future-past.

Existentialism claims that it is fundamental to what we are to want to be at one with ourselves, to *be* what we are instead of having always to strive to be it, to achieve a future state of total completion in which we no longer lack anything. But we never arrive at this godlike state of total smug self-satisfaction because we never arrive at the future. Tomorrow all the pubs will have free beer, but as even the least philosophically minded person knows, tomorrow never comes. To which we can add, and yesterday is just a memory, even if its consequences have a way of coming back to haunt us.

Is all this a cause for regret and despair? Well, it shouldn't be, certainly not according to existentialism. For existentialism, it is just the way things are, and the way things are is the price you pay for existing as a conscious being at all. After all, you can't be conscious without being temporalized, without hurtling on through time like a truck with brake failure. Consciousness is inconceivable other than as temporal. In fact, as I've been more than hinting, time and consciousness are almost the same thing.

Existentialism recommends bravely accepting that this is how life is and making the most of it. It recommends building your life on the firm basis of hard, uncomfortable truths rather than the shifting sands of soft, comfortable delusions. Ironically perhaps, there is also the suggestion that people will actually be happier and relatively more satisfied if they accept what the endless temporal flight of consciousness towards the future implies, namely, that it is alien to the human condition for a person to be completely satisfied and contented for any length of time. If people genuinely accept this truth of the human condition and take it to heart they will cease to hanker after complete fulfilment and total happiness, or at least be far less disappointed and far more calm and philosophical about life when complete fulfilment and total happiness are not achieved. Existentialism offers satisfaction of a stoical kind through the acceptance of the inevitability of a certain amount of dissatisfaction.

The most important consequence of the theory that consciousness is essentially temporal concerns freedom. It is because consciousness is essentially temporal that it is essentially free. I'll get into the details of exactly why this is later when I come to look at freedom and responsibility, but the key point to keep in mind for now is that we are free precisely because we are not fixed in the present. Only a temporal being can be free because to be free is to have possibilities and genuine alternatives *in the future*. We are our future possibilities and our freedom consists in being free towards the future, but as I say, more about freedom later.

For now, we need to look at another perennial existential truth of the human condition, namely, the existence of other people. More precisely, we need to investigate what de Beauvoir, Sartre and other existentialist philosophers call our *being-for-others*.

Being-for-others

Each of us is what Sartre and his gang call a being-for-itself. Not only are people conscious of the world, they are conscious of themselves as conscious of the world. This self-consciousness or self-reflection is a defining feature of human beings. Only monkeys, dolphins and octopi (creepy) have anything approaching it. Each person is a being for him or her self. However deluded a person may actually be about himself he feels he knows himself, he is the measure of himself, the judge and jury of his thoughts and actions. He experiences himself as free, as creating himself moment by moment through the things he chooses to do and the paths he chooses to take. He transcends the world in an almost godlike way and it is as though the world were there for him alone, his oyster, his playground. So much for being-for-itself. Being-for-itself is, as you may have already guessed, only half the picture.

People are seldom if ever truly alone, especially these days with the world population spiralling out of control and everywhere getting so crowded. Each person constantly confronts the existence of other people, not simply as *objects* in his world, but as *subjects* who see him and judge him and reduce him to an object in their world. To be an object in the world of the Other, to *be* for the Other, to *be* in danger of being belittled by the Other, this is the meaning of *being-for-others*.

'The Other', by the way, is a fancy existentialist term for another person, particularly one who looks at me, sees me and has opinions about me that put me in my place. As you may already be thinking, the term 'the Other' is rather pretentious. Nobody comes back from town saying 'Hello Dear, I had many encounters with *the Other* while I was shopping'. To be fair though, the term allows for ease of explanation when discussing the various aspects of the phenomenon of being-for-others and the complex interplay of objectivity and subjectivity that occurs when this person encounters that person at the shops, in the park, in the mountains or anywhere else.

To get a better sense of what being-for-others is and the whole subject to object thing that takes place when the Other appears on the scene consider the following example:

A man called John is walking all alone in the wilds down a beautiful valley beside a rushing stream. He drinks in the fresh air and the stunning scenery and feels he is master of all he surveys. He is a pure godlike subject presiding over mountains, rocks, rivers and lakes, over every tree, flower and blade of grass. John feels he is at the centre of the world, that it is all arranged for him alone, that it exists only from his point of view. Rounding a large boulder that towers over him John suddenly catches sight of a stranger in the distance walking up the valley towards him. With deep irritation and disappointment John realizes it is the dreaded Other. Even though the Other hasn't seen John yet the presence of the Other immediately affects John's situation. The appearance of the Other signifies the disintegration of the world from John's point of view. The whole vast situation, which was John's to judge and evaluate as he wished, contains a new source of judgements and values which are not his and which escape him. John was the centre of the world but now the Other has decentralized him. The world is re-orientated towards the Other and meanings unknown to John flow in the direction of the Other.

The Other, as Sartre so flatteringly puts it, is a *drain-hole* down which John's world flows. The very appearance of the Other prevents John from playing God. He ceases to be the centre and sole judge of all he surveys because a source of re-evaluation has appeared on the scene to steal his world away from him and with it his splendid godlike transcendence. A wilderness where a person enjoying solitude encounters another person can certainly feel far more crowded than a busy street.

The Other hasn't seen John yet. Although he is a drain-hole in John's world, a big threat to John's centralization, he is still an object in John's world. But the Other is walking up the valley and it is only a matter of time before John is seen by the Other and becomes an object in his world. The Other draws near and soon John sees the Other see him. In knowing he is seen John becomes uncomfortably aware of himself as an object, of the clothes he is wearing and the way he is wearing them, of the way he is walking and the expression on his face. As he draws near to the Other he checks his flies, dons a watery smile and prepares himself to deliver that awkward, non-threatening hello and banal comment on the weather that strangers feel obliged to exchange when passing in the middle of nowhere. The Other, who might also be called John, does the same.

John feels relieved when he has passed the Other, less awkwardly aware of himself as an object. Released from the possessive gaze of the Other he begins to relax and to reclaim the wilderness. Soon the Other will round the large boulder and vanish and the world will become John's kingdom once more.

Even when a person is physically alone, miles from the shops, miles from anywhere and anyone, other people are likely to be in his thoughts. Even if, unlike most of us, he is not particularly paranoid, he may well be plagued by the actual and imagined judgements of others and be unable to stop thinking about what others think of him, of the tactless things he said at the staff meeting or the idiotic things he did at the office party. In his embarrassment he can't help thinking that the Other has somehow got hold of a part of him, trapped him, got the better of him. The Other makes him into something he feels he is not, something he does not want to recognize or feel responsible for. Against his will, in opposition to his freedom and his joyful transcendence, other people force him to *be* what he is for them rather than what he is for himself.

Being-for-others is a central theme in all of Sartre's fictional writing and not least in his novel, *The Age of Reason*. Most of the characters in *The Age of Reason* suffer a sense of enslavement to the opinion of others to a lesser or greater extent. Its central character, a cynical philosophy professor called Mathieu Delarue, feels enslaved by the opinion of his girlfriend, Marcelle, when he leaves her house after she has told him she is pregnant with his child. 'He stopped, transfixed: it wasn't true, he wasn't alone. Marcelle had not let him go: she was thinking of him, and this is what she thought: "The dirty dog, he's let me down." It was no use striding along the dark, deserted street, anonymous, enveloped in his garments – he could not escape her' (*The Age of Reason*, p. 19).

So, each person suffers his being-for-others in shame, embarrassment or humiliation, though sometimes in pride as well. As doom merchants, existentialist philosophers are a bit slow to admit there is also an upside to being-for-others. Shame, embarrassment, humiliation, pride, dignity, these are all aspects of what makes a fully rounded person. They are essentially *other-related* aspects. They are me but they exist *over there* for the Other. Although there is also what Sartre calls 'the religious practice of shame' (*Being and Nothingness*, p. 245), feeling ashamed before God or the all seeing eye of your deceased grandmother, these are derivative forms of shame. Shame is essentially shame before someone. Nobody feels ashamed or proud all alone.

A person is his being-for-others – his shame, his pride – but he is it out there for the Other. The Other possesses part of what a person is and is free to judge him; free to admire, respect or despise him. Having aspects of his being belong to others, aspects that he is nonetheless held responsible for, makes a person uncomfortable. A good deal of most people's behaviour is directed towards seeking to influence their being-for-others, or even to gain complete control over it. People generally desire to impress and certainly go to great lengths to encourage other people to love, respect or fear them. People talk about feeling good in themselves and about setting *personal* goals, but really they are all shouting, 'Look at me, I'm so beautiful, so clever, so hard, so cool. I exist, I exist. Even if I'm not better than you, I'm just as good as you in my own way.' Those with ability and determination do it by winning Olympic gold medals or qualifying as doctors. Those with less talent do it by learning to juggle, having tattoos or wheel spinning their car at traffic lights. As many great philosophers and religious teachers have noted down through the centuries, 'All is vanity.'

If this isn't true then why doesn't billionaire Virgin boss, Richard Branson, for example, just fly his balloons around the world, or whatever it is he does, without banging on about it to anyone who will listen? He doesn't need the money that publicity brings so why all the self-promotion? And, to be really cynical, vanity is what much of the current obsession with doing daft stunts for charity is all about. Charity gives people the opportunity to show off and publicize their achievements, usually their ability to run a marathon dressed as a chicken or Homer Simpson, while they hide behind a veil of false modesty and a charade of philanthropy.

I'm forced to question my own motives in writing this book. Sure, I want to perform a sort of intellectual duty by telling you how to be an existentialist, but only so I can flaunt my ability to write another book – dressed as a chicken for all you know – and in so doing triumph over people who haven't written as many books as I have, especially all those bastards who have put me down in the past. Unfortunately, as people who write books on how to be an existentialist don't make it on to Saturday night TV chat shows, I will remain obscure; a person detached from the name on the cover, a name that, incidentally, I share with several other writers anyway. Perhaps I should have chosen another means of showing off but I lack the talent for anything else. I was going to add, 'and I probably lack the talent for this too', but that would just be more false modesty and covert vanity.

Have you ever thought that modesty and shyness are just very crafty ways of getting attention? Like those deeply irritating people you meet who talk very quietly. They think they are so bloody important that they can deliver their gems of wisdom in a whisper while everyone else around them must lean in and strain to hear what they have to say.

There was a boy at my school called Ray Groves who could speak perfectly well but never would. He spoke only to his family by all accounts. He was, to give him his due, amazingly good at keeping it up. Teachers usually scream at kids to keep quiet, but over the years I saw several teachers scream at Ray to speak. Although I admired his stubbornness, I never saw Ray's refusal to speak as a mark of shyness, reserve or sensitivity. I just saw him as covertly arrogant and utterly self-centred. I didn't know these words at junior school but they certainly capture how I felt about Ray. He took words from people but never gave any back. It made people want to talk to him, made them think that he had something interesting to say. Whereas, if he had spoken, people may have realized he was a bore with nothing to say worth listening to.

Like most people I am full of resentment about other people. I even feel resentment for a little kid I once knew at school who some said never spoke simply because he was ashamed of his squeaky little voice. I resent Ray Groves because, though I tried, he judged me as not good enough to speak to. Resentment is a feature of and a reaction to being-for-others, the fact that the Other can so easily clip our wings and bring us down.

Try as they might, people can never be sure they are creating the desired impression, that others are not freely choosing to adopt an opinion of them contrary to the opinion they wish them to have. I have managed here to form contrary opinions about such relatively decent characters as charity fundraisers, people who talk quietly and people who refuse to talk at all. Even if people are pretty sure others are impressed, that others love, admire or fear them and so on, they can never be certain it will last. Each person's freedom is subject to the freedom of the Other, the transcendence of the Other. The mere gaze of the Other fixes a person as an object in the world of the Other. As an object for the Other a person is a *transcendence-transcended* by the transcendence of the Other. He ceases to exist primarily as a free subject for himself and exists instead primarily as an un-free object for others.

To make better sense of the switch from transcendent subject to transcended object take the example of a man looking at pornography. Until the man is caught in the act he remains a free being-in-the-world, a transcendence. He is a subject absorbed in what he is doing and does not judge himself. He is free to transcend the meaning of his act and does not have to define himself as a bit of a pervert. Later on, if he reflects on his act, he can avoid branding himself a pervert by telling himself his act was simply an aberration and so on, a meaningless distraction with no bearing on his character or morals. Suddenly, however, he realizes he is being spied on. Suddenly, he is more exposed than the naked models he looks at. What he is is now revealed to the Other and thereby to himself. All at once his act, which for him had little or no meaning, has escaped him and acquired meaning for the Other. It now belongs to the Other for whom he has become an obscene object.

In catching him in the act the Other has caught his freedom and ᵢₛ ᵢₛ
liberty to judge him as he pleases, to inflict meanings upon him –
voyeur, pervert, dirty old man, fellow connoisseur.

It must always be kept in mind when considering being-for-others
that a person is Other for the Other and is therefore able to alienate
the freedom of the Other in turn by transcending his transcendence.
Controversially, existentialist philosophers tend to characterize human
relationships as a ceaseless power struggle for domination and transcendence, arguing that the basis of all human relationships is *conflict*.
This conflict, and the suffering that results from having a being-for-others that is beyond a person's control, is explored most famously and
thoroughly in Sartre's monumentally pessimistic play, *In Camera*.
Although thoroughly depressing and claustrophobic, *In Camera* is a very
clever play about three nasty, self-centred people trapped in a living
room for ever – a bit like *Big Brother* only with intelligent conversation.
Garcin, one of the central characters of the play, famously exclaims,
'There's no need for red-hot pokers. Hell is other people!' (*In Camera*,
p. 223).

Some critics resist the claim made by many existentialist philosophers
that the essence of all human relationships is conflict, that hell is other
people, not because they think it is pessimistic, but because they think
it is a sweeping generalization that does not stand up to close scrutiny.
They argue that existentialist philosophers like de Beauvoir, Camus and
Sartre speak too much from their own miserable personal experiences.
Being in their prime around the time of World War II and associating
almost exclusively with a bunch of spiteful Parisian intellectuals obsessed
with criticizing each other for effect, led them to conclude that all people spend their entire lives at variance with each other trying to do each
other down. For sure, people are very often at each other's throats, and
anyone who lived through the horrors of World War II might be forgiven
for concluding that conflict is universal. Nonetheless, it seems fair to say
that existentialist philosophers too often over-emphasize one aspect of
human behaviour for dramatic effect. When they suggest that what

Sartre calls *the look* is always threatening, they ignore the evidence of certain contrary situations, such as, for example, the caring, protective-protected look between mother and child. The real truth seems to be that other people are sometimes hell, sometimes heaven.

To be fair to existentialist philosophers it should be noted that they do in fact show some appreciation of the capacity people have for being together without conflict in their notion of *Mitsein* – German for 'being-with'. The French existentialist philosophers followed the German existentialist philosopher, Heidegger, in using the term 'Mitsein' to refer to the phenomenon of being-*with*-others; to the phenomenon of 'we'. On those occasions when a *we* vibe takes over a person is not transcended by other people, nor does he seek to transcend other people. Rather, his ego is transcended by some collective experience or enterprise in which he becomes submerged in an *us*.

This submergence in an *us*, however, is often maintained through conflict with a *them* as opponent or hate object – conflict at the group level. Heidegger's own experience of the *Mitsein* was as a member of Hitler's National Socialist Party. Even so, there are occasions when the *us* does not require a *them* in order to be maintained. For example, a group may work together on a task with a common goal that is not primarily the goal of beating or destroying the competition. Alternatively, a group united together by religion, music, dancing or drugs, or all of these highs simultaneously, may achieve a state of reverie or synergy amounting to a collective loss of egoism. Pure heaven.

Freedom and responsibility

Like Mel Gibson in that wonderful if not entirely historically accurate film, *Braveheart*, existentialist philosophers are always banging on about freedom. Even when they are not liberating Scotland from the English (or France from the Germans) or being hung, drawn and quartered, they consider human freedom to be of the utmost importance. William Wallace, the hero played by Gibson, is a tough freedom fighter who will just not be dictated to, especially after the English scum who occupy his bonny Scotland slit his wife's throat. He recognizes the existential truth that he is not only free when the powers that be allow him a few privileges (not that they ever do), but that he is fundamentally and inalienably free whatever his circumstances, that nobody can in fact take his freedom away from him however much they try to enslave him. Like a true existentialist he is wise enough to recognize that whatever he does he chooses to do it, that he is always responsible for his actions. Moreover, like a true existentialist he insists on affirming and asserting his freedom. He refuses to choose himself as the slave his English oppressors want him to be, and in refusing to use his freedom to check his freedom he pays the ultimate price. Victorious at first, his army is finally defeated and he is captured. His limbs are posted to the four corners of the realm but they are the limbs of a man who dies asserting his *FREEDOM*.

Although most existentialist philosophers are interested in civil liberties and human rights, their advocacy of human freedom is not just a political stance, a desire to promote liberty and justice around the world, it is deeply philosophical. Existentialist philosophers hold on considered philosophical grounds that all people are fundamentally, necessarily and inalienably free regardless of their circumstances or the level of political, social and economic oppression they suffer. Contrary to popular belief, the existentialist philosophy of freedom is not primarily concerned with liberty. For existentialist philosophers freedom is not essentially about what people are at liberty to do, about what they are able to do or allowed to do and so on, but about each person's *responsibility* for whatever they do or do not do in every circumstance in which they find themselves. It is vital to a proper understanding of the existentialist theory of personal freedom to realize that it is just as much a theory of personal responsibility. Freedom is not freedom from responsibility, freedom is having to make choices and therefore having to take responsibility.

The existentialist theory of freedom is rooted in the existentialist theory of choice and action which in turn is rooted in the existentialist theory of human consciousness and temporality we looked at earlier. In arguing for free will existentialist philosophers do not simply make room for it by offering various arguments against determinism. Determinism being the view that all events and states are necessitated by prior events and states. They offer a positive account of free will showing not only that free will is possible, but that it is necessary given the nature of consciousness.

As seen, consciousness is a paradoxical, ambiguous and indeterminate being that is never at one with itself, never identical with itself. As a *relationship* to the world it is not founded upon itself but upon what it is not, and is therefore nothing in itself, nothing in the present. Consciousness is never in the present. It exists only as a perpetual temporal flight or transcendence away from the past towards the future. As a temporal transcendence towards the future consciousness stands outside the causal order, the world of cause and effect events.

Events, which are what they are and can never be other than what they are once they have happened, belong to a past that exists for a consciousness that is the future of that past. The past exists only for a consciousness that transcends it towards the future. Consciousness exists only as a transcendence of the past towards the future. Consciousness is the future of the past, which is to say, it is the future *possibilities* of the past. As nothing but a being towards the future, as nothing but the future possibilities of what it transcends, consciousness has to be these possibilities. It cannot not be an opening up of possibilities.

This stuff about time and possibility is a key part of existentialism that is hard to put more simply. Don't worry if the last paragraph skimmed over your head hardly making contact with your hair or your bald patch, just read it again! Re-reading in philosophy is quite normal. It is a wise habit rather than a sign of limited brain cells. What? You've already re-read it five times and it's still as clear as mud? No worries. Move on. I'm sure you'll get the general gist. The brain is more like the stomach than people think. It needs time to digest things and it may well be that the general gist will come to you later on when you've put this book down, when you are out jogging, eating your supper or watching TV. The general gist of a thing often comes to me when I'm in the shower, not the most convenient place if I want to make notes. Interestingly, it's often when we get right away from pens, paper and books that we do our best thinking.

Anyway, the general gist of what I'm saying here is that we are able to be free in a world of mechanical cause and effect events because we constantly escape that mechanical world towards the future. It is in the future at which we aim that we are free.

The freedom of consciousness consists in the perpetual opening up of the possibilities of situations. Consciousness discovers itself in a world of possibilities that it creates by being a temporal transcendence towards the future. Consciousness is not *in* the future, the future exists only as the 'not yet' towards which consciousness flees. Furthermore, the future can never be reached because to 'reach' the future is to immediately render it past. Nonetheless, it is in the future at which consciousness aims that consciousness is free, free in the sense of having a range of future possibilities which it realizes for itself.

By choosing among its possibilities, by choosing a course of action, consciousness brings some of its possibilities into actuality and abandons others. The transformation of possibility into actuality is the transformation of what existentialist philosophers call *future-past* into *past-future*. As we've seen, the past is a past-future, a one-time future that has now passed into the past. Some of the possibilities that comprise consciousness get transformed into a past-future and this past-future immediately becomes the launch pad for a further transcendence by consciousness towards new future possibilities. And so on and on the process goes until death makes heroes of us all.

The fact that consciousness has to be a temporal transcendence in order to exist at all, the fact that it cannot not be an opening up of possibilities, implies that it cannot not be free. It is a necessary feature of human consciousness that it is not free to cease being free. People are necessarily free, or, as Sartre puts it, people are 'condemned to be free' (*Being and Nothingness*, p. 462).

A person can never surrender his freedom. He can never make himself an object causally determined by the physical world because the very project of surrender, the very attempt to render himself causally determined, must be a free choice of himself. A person cannot make himself determined by the world, for whenever or however he attempts to do it, he must *choose* to do it. A person can never not choose because, as Sartre says, 'Not to choose is, in fact, to choose not to choose' (*Being and Nothingness*, p. 503). A person's freedom does not consist in a complete detachment from all obligations, a sort of hippy freedom, it consists in the constant responsibility of having to choose who he is through the actions he chooses to perform in response to the adversity and resistance of his situation. In the opinion of hard-line existentialist philosophers there is no end to the responsibility of having to choose.

It is important to note that existentialist philosophers call the adversity and resistance of things and situations *facticity*. Facticity is what freedom works to overcome, although freedom always needs facticity in order to be the overcoming of it. As Simone de Beauvoir puts it, 'The resistance of the thing [facticity] sustains the action of man [freedom] as air sustains the flight of the dove' (*The Ethics of Ambiguity*, p. 81). In so far as freedom is very closely linked to what we have been calling *transcendence*, we can say that transcendence is the transcendence of facticity. Transcendence and facticity exist in close relation to one another; they give each other meaning and reality. 'Transcendence' and 'facticity' are very useful philosophical terms that allow existentialist philosophers to launch into various subtle descriptions about the relationships people have with their own bodies, with the world, with each other and so on. This will be seen when we come to look at bad faith in the chapter on how *not* to be an existentialist. Bad faith is a kind of game in which transcendence and facticity are deliberately muddled up and confused.

Freedom and disability

Just as freedom is necessary, so it is also limitless. Not limitless in the sense that a person is free to do anything, fly unaided, walk on water or lick his elbow, but limitless in the sense that his obligation to be free, his obligation to choose a response in every situation, is unremitting. Even if a person is disabled and unable to walk, for example, his freedom is still unlimited. He is not free to walk in the sense of being at liberty to walk, but he is still free to choose the meaning of his disability and hence responsible for his response to it. Controversially, Sartre says, 'I can not be crippled without choosing myself as crippled. This means that I choose the way in which I constitute my disability (as "unbearable," "humiliating," "to be hidden," "to be revealed to all," "an object of pride," "the justification for my failures," *etc*.)' (*Being and Nothingness*, p. 352). If a disabled person considers his disability the ruination of his life then that is a choice he has made for which he alone is responsible. He is free to choose his disability positively. To strive, for example, to be a successful para-athlete or to spend the time he used to spend playing football writing a book or fundraising.

The Hollywood actor, Christopher Reeve, who played Superman in the movies, was paralysed from the neck down in a horse riding accident in 1995. By a sustained act of will worthy of Superman himself Reeve refused to be ruined by his quadriplegia. He remained positive and active and campaigned tirelessly for the rights of disabled people, raising tens of millions of dollars for research into paralysis. Reeve died young as a result of his paralysis, but that's not the point. Everyone dies sooner or later. The point is how he lived his life. He once said, 'I think that setting challenges is a great motivator, because too many people with disabilities allow that to become the dominating factor in their lives, and I refuse to allow a disability to determine how I live my life.' I don't know if Reeve was a student of existentialism but he certainly had some of the qualities that make a true existentialist.

I recently climbed Mt. Snowdon in North Wales. Half way up I passed a man inching his way down the mountain on elbow crutches.

⌡ a hunchback and his lower legs were so splayed that he walked
ɘ sides of his feet. I nodded hello as I trudged past aiming for the
top, wondering how he had got there. On my way down nearly two
hours later I caught up with him less than a mile from where I had first
seen him and we walked down together for a while. His condition
made every small step he took down the mountain a major task. He
was obliged to individually negotiate with painful slowness each rock
that made up the rough path and his progress was as dangerous as it
was slow as his crutches occasionally slipped on wet rocks or sank in
mud. He had little power to save himself from falling and had fallen
several times. It emerged that he had spina bifida. As it was physically
impossible for him to climb up mountains he had taken the train to the
top of Snowdon and set himself the awesome challenge of walking
down. It would take him many exhausting hours to descend the five
mile Llanberis Path on his deformed legs and his elbow crutches but he
was determined to do it. Despite the difficulty and the pain he was
enjoying himself and would accept no help. He was happy to be
mastering the situation in which he had placed himself, happy to be
mastering his disability and choosing its meaning.

I found myself comparing him to couch-potatoes I know, who through
greed, laziness and general self-neglect, have made themselves unhealthy
and hugely overweight. They would struggle to get down Snowdon
almost as much as the man with spina bifida, except that they wouldn't
bother to attempt the hike in the first place. It would definitely be a
return ticket on the mountain railway for those slobs. It made me wonder, who in this world is really disabled? The 'cripple' who always chooses
to push himself and do as much as he can, or the lazy, obese person who
always chooses the soft option and does as little as possible except when
it comes to eating crap and making excuses? Perhaps the only truly
disabled people in this world are those who have a disabling attitude.

To insist that a disabled person is, existentially speaking, responsible
for his disability, is certainly a tough and uncompromising view. It even
seems harsh and politically incorrect in our contemporary excuse culture that consistently undervalues individual responsibility and consist-

ently overvalues the blaming of circumstances and facticity. This view should, however, be seen as empowering and very much politically correct in terms of the respect it shows disabled people. To tell a so-called disabled person that he is, existentially speaking, responsible for his disability, is not to insult him or to show him a callous lack of consideration, it is to inspire him and to offer him the only real hope available if his disability is incurable. Any disabled person who is not wallowing in self-pity – *choosing* to wallow in self-pity as Sartre would have it – would surely embrace Sartre's description of his situation. No disabled person wants to be reduced to their disability; considered as 'just a quadriplegic in a wheelchair' or 'just a spastic on crutches'. Sartre is saying precisely that a disabled person is not his disability but instead his freely chosen response to his disability and his transcendence of it.

The man I met on Snowdon with spina bifida was not disabled but definitely *differently able*. He was doing the utmost the facticity of his body allowed him to do; a damned sight more than some people without his congenital disadvantages can be bothered to do. I got back to my hotel at the foot of Snowdon, showered then went out for a well deserved cup of tea. All afternoon and into the evening, looking up at the mountains, I wondered if he was still descending at his snail's pace. I guess he got down OK and I never heard anything to the contrary, but if he died trying then he died transcending the awful facticity of his so-called disability. A good death I guess. Unlike a lot of public buildings, existentialism has always been equipped for disabled access, although, on the other hand, it offers the disabled no special concessions.

Possible limits to freedom

More moderate existentialists like Maurice Merleau-Ponty, whose great contribution to existentialism is a book called *Phenomenology of*

Perception, think that there are sometimes limitations to freedom. Of course, people do sometimes do things over which they have no control, like vomit after drinking fifteen bottles of beer – beer they chose to drink in the first place of course – but this is not really the kind of thing Merleau-Ponty has in mind. Vomiting after drinking fifteen bottles of beer is not really something that a person does, so much as something that just happens with his out of control body. Although, having said that, some people are able to hold down fifteen bottles of beer a lot longer than other people through sheer will power. Merleau-Ponty is thinking more of certain dispositions and responses that require conscious awareness in order to occur but are nevertheless not matters of choice. Vomiting doesn't necessarily require conscious awareness. People, mainly rock stars, often vomit in their sleep with dire consequences – Jimi Hendrix, John Bonham, Bon Scott. Philosophers who sympathize with Merleau-Ponty's position list sense of humour, sexual preference, panic reactions and insanity as examples of dispositions and responses that require conscious awareness in order to occur but are not matters of choice. A quick examination of these examples does appear to reveal that not every conscious response is freely chosen.

Sense of humour: Although education and experience can change a person's sense of humour over time, if he finds a joke funny at the time he hears it he is not choosing to find it funny. So, if you find the deliberately and outrageously offensive English stand-up comedian Bernard Manning funny, go ahead, laugh it up, it isn't your fault. Actually, I find Bernard Manning funny partly because he reminds me of all those sanctimonious, right-minded, politically correct liberals who have taught themselves to find him offensive. Part of what I find amusing is their offence, but I'm not sure this point is relevant to the current debate.

Sexual preference: Although sane people are undoubtedly responsible for all actions that stem from their sexual preferences they are not responsible for their sexual preferences. They do not choose them and can not choose to change them. On a genuinely serious note, we might ask why some psychologists think they can counsel paedophiles out of their sexual preference? Do they think they can counsel heterosexuals and homosexuals out of theirs? Some paedophiles have asked to be castrated in order to stop them from doing what they do. In making this request they are conveniently confusing a sexual preference for which they are not responsible with actions for which they are certainly responsible, their intention being to cunningly evade responsibility for what they do.

Panic reactions: Panic has both a physical and a mental dimension. It is a physical response that requires consciousness in order to be made, but it is not always under the control of consciousness. Sometimes panic overwhelms consciousness. It produces a fight-or-flight reaction which freezes a person between engaging the enemy or legging it. He remains starkly conscious but he has temporarily lost control of himself. The fact that a soldier, for example, can eventually learn to gain control over his panic reactions through training and experience, and hence place himself in a position to be able to choose not to panic, does not imply that every soldier, particularly the rookie, has the choice of whether or not to panic on a particular occasion when the bullets start flying and the big guns start blazing.

Insanity: Psychiatrists recognize that the genuinely mentally disturbed have obsessive, compulsive tendencies over which they have little or no control. The hard-line existentialist theory of freedom does not allow for the diminished responsibility that is the accepted hallmark of mental illness.

It is surely correct to argue that responsibility can not be avoided or freedom limited by choosing not to choose. And certainly helplessness in many if not most situations in life is an all too familiar sham. It appears, however, to be wrong to argue that people are *always* responsible for what they do and the evaluations they make. Of all the existentialist philosophers, Sartre probably has the toughest and most uncompromising theory of freedom and responsibility. To some extent it is a result of the historical period in which it was produced. Sartre, his thoughts increasingly influenced by political concerns, did his bit to resist the rising tide of fascism and Nazism that culminated in World War II by arguing in favour of individual freedom and inalienable personal responsibility.

Perhaps, in the end, Sartre is not offering us a philosophical theory worked out in every single detail so much as an ideal to aspire to through sheer unrelenting will power and implacable bloody mindedness – a life of maximum responsibility and minimum excuses. Or would you rather aspire to be a whinging, irresponsible slob? There is a surprisingly large amount of public funding available for people with the latter aspiration.

Freedom and anxiety

A person's awareness of his unlimited or nearly unlimited freedom can be a source of anxiety or anguish. It can make a person anxious to know there is nothing that he is in the manner of *being* it, that whatever he does is his free choice, that there is nothing to stop him from pulling whatever crazy stunt he thinks of pulling other than his choice not to pull it. A friend of mine once stuck his foot in the front spokes of a bicycle he was riding. Later on at the hospital when I asked him why on earth he had done it he replied that it was simply because the spokes were there in front of him and because he wanted to. To his existentialist credit he didn't make excuses and say, 'I had this over-whelming urge that "made me" do it.'

Our freedom makes us anxious because there is nothing but our freedom itself to stop us from performing destructive, dangerous, embarrassing or disreputable acts at any moment. You could choose right now to tell your boss, if you have one, to eat shit, or you could destroy your respectable reputation in an instant by choosing to expose your private parts in the street. Obviously I don't recommend it, but like an infinity of other possible actions we don't perform each moment, it's always an option. Rather than write the next paragraph I could leap out of my window. . . .

Obviously I didn't leap because here is the next paragraph. But you could leap out of your window rather than read on. Obviously, for fear of litigation at the hands of our excuse culture (our 'blame anyone but yourself' culture) I must stress that I'm not recommending it. Still, existentially speaking, the choice is yours.

Sartre distinguishes what can be called *freedom-anxiety* from fear. He takes the example of a man picking his way carefully along a narrow precipice (*Being and Nothingness*, pp. 53–56). The man fears he might fall but he also suffers anxiety, which manifests itself as vertigo, because he is free to jump. Sartre says: 'Vertigo is anguish to the extent that I am afraid not of falling over the precipice, but of throwing myself over' (*Being and Nothingness*, p. 53).

In order to avoid freedom-anxiety people often adopt strategies to convince themselves and others that they are not free, that they need not or cannot choose, or have not chosen when in fact they have. In the case of the precipice walker, he quite understandably strives to ignore the freedom to jump that menaces him by absorbing himself in the task of picking his way cautiously along the path as though his movements were physically determined by the demands of the situation rather than by himself. He imagines himself compelled to act as he does by survival instincts and so on.

To deny the reality of freedom and choice, perhaps as a means of avoiding anxiety, perhaps as a coping strategy, perhaps with the aim of relinquishing responsibility, is what existentialist philosophers call *bad faith*. Bad faith is not the opposite of freedom, it is freedom that gives rise directly to the possibility of bad faith in so far as bad faith is a project of freedom where freedom aims at its own suppression and denial. Joke: A student goes to see his Existentialism lecturer. 'Are you free?' the student asks, poking his head around the door. 'Yes,' replies the lecturer, 'but I don't want to be'. If you want to be a true existentialist then you have to strive to *want* to be free, to assert your freedom and avoid bad faith at every turn. The next chapter is all about bad faith.

3 How Not to Be an Existentialist

A person can fail to be an existentialist by not knowing anything about existentialism, by knowing about it but failing to believe a word of it or by making no effort to live the life it recommends. Hopefully, having read this far, you now know a fair bit about existentialism and thanks to its candid assessment of the human condition have been persuaded that it is largely true. If this is your position then you have satisfied criteria 1 and 2 of being an existentialist that I set out at the beginning of Chapter 1. So, you are well on your way to becoming an existentialist having crossed off two of the three criteria. As the much maligned Captain William Bligh once said (at least in a movie I saw), 'Always think how far you've come, not how far you have to go.' This was his positive way of telling his long-suffering crew there was still a long way to go, just as telling you about him is my positive way of telling you there is still a long way to go.

Following the mutiny on the *Bounty* in 1789, Bligh was set adrift in a 23ft open launch with 18 crew members and not much else. For 47 days he navigated the launch 3,618 nautical miles to the island of Timor with nothing but a sextant, a pocket watch and barrel loads of Royal Navy determination, toughness and true grit. I don't think Bligh was an existentialist and I don't know enough about him to know if he was authentic, but he certainly exhibited some of the personal qualities required to be an existentialist. A sour-faced old git by all accounts – not actually one of the personal qualities required to be an existentialist but it may help – he stared his grim reality square in the face and asked himself, 'What is required here?' And then he went and did it. He didn't do his best, doing your best is for infants on school sports day, for little people who don't really know what their best is, he did what was *necessary*.

Knowing what existentialism is is relatively easy, believing it is easier still. In fact, believing it involves no effort at all. Just sit back and let an honest appraisal of life convince you. The hard part, a part as hard as navigating a tiny launch across thousands of miles of hostile ocean, is satisfying criteria 3 as set out at the beginning of Chapter 1. That is, striving with some success to live and act according to the findings and recommendations of existentialism. As existentialism itself claims, theory is all well and good but in the end it's *actions* that count. Learning about existentialism is probably easier than using a sextant to measure the angular distance of a celestial object above the horizon, but *being* an existentialist is probably harder than navigating across the pacific in a rowing boat with nothing but 18 scurvy sailors and a shiver of sharks for company.

By far the biggest obstacle or pit fall on the voyage to being a true existentialist is *bad faith*. To act in bad faith is the most sure fire way of failing to be an existentialist. Presumably, you are reading this book because you want to know *how* to be an existentialist, not because you want to know how *not* to be an existentialist. Still, I think it will help you make huge advances towards your goal of becoming an existentialist if I describe how not to be an existentialist. That is, if I describe and analyse the bad faith behaviours you must avoid at all costs if you want to succeed.

The existentialist philosopher with the most to say about bad faith is good old Jean-Paul Sartre. The existentialist theory of bad faith is largely Sartre's theory, maybe the most interesting and thought provoking theory that ever came out of his great, brainy head. Sartre is obsessed with bad faith because it is so widespread and right at the heart of the way most people behave most of the time. Certainly, Sartre felt he was surrounded by bad faith during his stuffy, respectable middle-class childhood and writing about it at such length in his critiques, stories, novels, plays and biographies is his way of resisting it and rebelling against it, his way of getting us to do the same. It seems fair to say that to become a true existentialist a person has to learn to hate bad faith as much as Sartre does. Sartre and the theory of bad faith are so bound up with each other that it is impossible to examine bad faith without examining what Sartre has to say about it, without looking in some detail at the fascinating examples he uses to explain it. Enough said by way of justifying the strong Sartrean flavour of this chapter, let's get rowing.

Bad faith is not self-deception

Bad faith is often described as self-deception, as lying to yourself, because superficially it appears to be self-deception. This description, however, is at best an over-simplification and at worst misleading and wrong. Bad faith cannot be self-deception for the simple reason that self-deception, in the sense of lying to yourself, is impossible. A person can no more succeed in lying to himself than he can get away with cheating while playing himself at chess. 'I wonder if I'll notice if I just sneak a couple of pawns off the board?' A person simply cannot cheat without knowing he is cheating. Whenever a person lies he knows he is doing it. As Sartre says, 'The essence of the lie implies in fact that the liar actually is in complete possession of the truth which he is hiding' (*Being and Nothingness*, p. 71).

A lie involves a deliberate attempt to mislead and relies on the fact that a person's own consciousness is a consciousness the Other is not directly conscious of. Lying requires there to be two externally related consciousnesses, a psychic duality of deceiver and deceived. Such a psychic duality cannot exist within the unity of a single consciousness. Consciousness is *translucent*, it is consciousness through and through and thoughts exist only in so far as a person is conscious of them.

In being translucent consciousness can not be compartmentalized with thoughts concealed from each other in different compartments.

In rejecting the existence of a psychic duality within the unity of a single consciousness Sartre rejects the famous distinction made by the famous Austrian psychoanalyst Sigmund Freud between conscious and unconscious. In trying to show the absurdity of Freud's position Sartre argues that consciousness would not be able to repress certain unwanted thoughts and imprison them in the unconscious without actually *knowing* what it was repressing. Sartre says, 'If we reject the language and the materialistic mythology of psychoanalysis, we perceive that the censor in order to apply its activity with discernment must know what it is repressing' (*Being and Nothingness*, p. 75). A no-necked, knuckle headed nightclub bouncer dressed up in his tuxedo and dickie-bow can't do his job unless he knows who he is supposed to be excluding. 'Ere, what's your name? Sexual Desire for Mother is it? Hold on, I'll see if you're on the guest list. Nah, sorry mate. Not tonight. You're barred.'

Sartre explains as forms of bad faith the attitudes and behaviours that Freud explains as products of a psychic duality within a single person. Bad faith does not require a psychic duality within a single person and it does not involve self-deception. As will be seen, bad faith is more like an ongoing project of *self-distraction* or *self-evasion* than self-deception.

As bad faith is not an abstract concept but a concrete, existential phenomenon – the attitude, disposition and way of behaving of real people in real situations – it is best to give an account of it using specific, concrete examples of people in bad faith. This is certainly Sartre's approach. His books are stuffed full with characters in bad faith, some of them striving to overcome it and achieve authenticity, most of them sinking further into it as their lives drag on.

Flirting and teasing

Sartre opens the detailed account of bad faith he gives in *Being and Nothingness* with the example of a flirtatious but naïve young woman and the guy who is trying to bed her. He, you get the feeling, is older than her, more experienced, maybe even a bit of a lounge lizard. The flirt takes the guy's various compliments and seemingly polite attentions at face value ignoring their sexual background. Finally, the guy takes hold of the young woman's hand, creating a situation that demands from her a decisive response, but she chooses to flirt, neither taking her hand away or acknowledging the implications of holding hands. She treats her hand as though it is not a part of herself, as though it is an object for which she is not responsible, and she treats her act of omission of leaving her hand in the hand of the man as though it is not an action.

The young woman knows her hand is held and what this implies but somehow she evades this knowledge, or rather she is the ongoing project of seeking to evade it and distract herself from it. She distracts herself from the meaning of her situation and the disposition of her limbs by fleeing herself towards the future. Each moment she aims to become a person beyond her situated self, a person who is not defined by her current situation. She aims to become a being that is what it is, an object like a table or a rock, yet one that is still conscious. Such a being would not be subject to the demands of the situation, it would not be *responsible*. It would not be obliged to choose and to act.

She aspires to abandon her hand, her whole body, to the past, hoping to leave it all behind her. Yet, in the very act of trying to abandon her body she recognizes that the situation of her body is like a demand to choose. To take the man's hand willingly or to withdraw, that is the choice that faces her. But she fails to meet this demand by instead choosing herself as a being that would-be beyond the requirement to choose. It is this *negative* choice that exercises and distracts her and stands in for the positive choice she knows her situation demands. She avoids making this positive choice by striving to choose herself as a person who has transcended her responsibility for her embodied, situated self. She strives to choose herself as a being that has escaped its facticity, escaped the complications and demands of its situation.

As we have seen, every human being is both an object and a subject, a facticity and a transcendence, or to be more precise, the transcendence *of* his or her facticity. There are various related forms of bad faith as revealed by the various concrete examples Sartre provides and all of them manipulate in some way the facticity-transcendence 'double property of the human being' (*Being and Nothingness*, p. 79). In essence, bad faith is the project of seeking to invert and/or separate facticity and transcendence. The flirt treats the facticity of her situation, in terms of which her choices of herself should be exercised, as though it has a transcendent power over her body. That is, she treats her facticity as though it is a transcendence. At the same time, she treats her transcendent consciousness as though it is its own transcendence; as though it is a transcendence-in-itself rather than the transcendence of the facticity of her situation. That is, she treats her transcendence as though it is a facticity.

It is strongly suggested in the example itself how the flirt ought to behave to avoid being in bad faith. If she had the intention of becoming a true existentialist, the intention of striving to be authentic, she would choose either to push the man's hand away and tell him to get lost, or hold his hand and take responsibility for encouraging him. Interestingly, to cease being in bad faith her outward behaviour, her bodily movement or lack of movement, need not be any different. Her attitude, however, what she confronts mentally and what she evades, makes all the difference between having her hand held and holding hands. To try to ignore that her hand is held and what this implies is weak minded and irresponsible. It is choosing not to choose. It is *negative* choice, though a choice all the same. To decide to consent to hold hands and to recognize that this will encourage further tentative advances by the man, is strong minded and responsible. It is, so to speak, choosing to choose. It is positive choice.

Being a true existentialist, practising authentic behaviour, can be as simple as this. As simple as the difference between having your hand held and holding hands. The difficulty with being a true existentialist, however, as I've already said, is keeping it up. The difficulty is producing responsible responses all the time across the widest possible range of circumstances, some of them far more difficult to handle with guts and without excuses than little moves in the mating game.

Of course, it may have already occurred to you that a flirt who consents to hold hands or takes her hand away is by definition not a flirt. However, we can imagine a woman, or a man, who knowingly holds hands, knowingly encourages the Other, but also knows that they have no intention of ever going further with the Other than holding hands. This person seems to be a different kind of flirt, a knowing flirt, a tease. A flirt who leads the Other up a very short garden path with only a wall at the end and definitely no gate into a dark and interesting alley; a flirt who knows her actions are a false sign, as opposed to a flirt like Sartre's flirt who evades thinking about what her actions imply.

Is the knowing flirt – the tease – less in bad faith than the evasive flirt? Arguably, she is not, because she is deliberately misleading the Other. She is not planning to *use* him in a sexual sense, but she is nonetheless using him in some game of her own. Perhaps she wants to get her revenge on men in general for the way one or more men have treated her in the past. Perhaps she has reasons to get her revenge on this person in particular. Whatever her motives, or lack of them, to use another person without their consent, to treat them as a mere means to one's own ends, is to fail to respect them as a free being.

It can be argued that just as it is authentic to respect and affirm one's own freedom, so it is authentic to respect and affirm the freedom of others. To fail to respect the freedom of others, as we do when we tease and tantalize them, is to fall into a certain kind of bad faith, it is to fail to be authentic. Authenticity, it appears, is not just a personal matter but also about how we relate to other people. So much so, perhaps, that ethical and moral behaviour can be identified as *other-related authenticity*.

Waiters, actors and attitudes

Another example from *Being and Nothingness* of a character in bad faith is the waiter. Using all his skills as a writer of fiction Sartre paints a vivid picture of the waiter in action. The waiter walks with a robotic stiffness, restraining his movements as if he were a machine. He steps too rapidly towards his customers, he is too eager and attentive. We get the clear impression that he is playing at being a waiter. One common view of Sartre's waiter is that he is in bad faith for endeavouring through his performance to deny his transcendence and become his facticity. In other words, he overacts his role as a waiter to convince himself and others that he is not a person but an object, a waiter-*thing*. As a waiter-*thing* he would escape his freedom and the anxiety it causes him and become a sort of robot waiter; an object made to be a waiter and nothing but a waiter. He aims to become *for himself* the object, the function, the transcendence-transcended that he often is for other people in his role as waiter. He strives to be at one with his own representation of himself, but the very fact that he has to represent to himself what he is means that he cannot *be* it.

Striving to be a thing in order to escape the responsibility of being free is certainly an identifiable and common enough form of bad faith. However, against this view of Sartre's waiter it has been argued by some Sartre nerds, including myself, that although the waiter certainly strives to be a waiter-*thing*, he is not in bad faith because the purpose of his striving is not to escape his freedom. Arguably, he is no more in bad faith for trying to be a waiter than an actor is in bad faith for trying to be James Bond. A close look at Sartre's description of the waiter reveals that, just like an actor, there is a definite sense in which he knows what he is doing. He acts with insincere or ironical intent, consciously – though not self-consciously – impersonating a waiter. As the expression goes, he is *tongue in cheek*. He is doing an impression of a waiter; a good impression that, like all good impressions, is more like whoever than whoever himself. He has become so good at it that it is like second nature to him.

To say that acting like a waiter is second nature to him is not to say that he believes he has become a waiter in the way that a rock is a rock. Rather, it is to say that he has become his performance in the sense that when he is absorbed in his performance he does not reflect that he is performing. Sartre says that the waiter 'plays with his condition in order to *realize* it' (*Being and Nothingness*, p. 82). In saying this he does not mean that he plays with his condition in order to become it, but that his condition is only ever realized as a playing with his condition. As we've seen, a person can not achieve identity with himself and become once and for always what he aims at becoming. The waiter can never *be* what he is, he can only ever play at being it.

It seems to follow from what has been said in the last couple of paragraphs that far from being in bad faith, the waiter Sartre describes is *authentic*, the very opposite of bad faith. Unlike the flirt he does not evade what he is – the transcendence *of* his facticity – by striving to treat his facticity as a transcendence and his transcendence as a facticity. Instead, he strives to take full responsibility for the reality of his situation, choosing himself positively in his situation by throwing himself wholeheartedly into his chosen role. He strives to embrace what Sartre calls in his *War Diaries*, his 'being-in-situation' (*War Diaries*, p. 54). A waiter in bad faith would be a reluctant, rueful waiter who kept on thinking, 'I'm not really a waiter.' He would be a waiter who *chose* to wait at tables while wishing he was someone else somewhere else.

I was a school teacher for ten years. For the first few years I endured it just for the money and more or less hated it most of the time. I kept thinking, this isn't me. But it was me because I was doing it. You can't claim you're a writer, a sports commentator, a movie star or anything else if what you actually do everyday is teach classes. I was in bad faith. To be authentic I needed either to throw myself into the role with sustained enthusiasm or find something else to do that I felt committed to doing. As I couldn't find anything else at the time that paid the bills so well as teaching I decided to throw myself into the teaching role with more passion. At first it wasn't easy but eventually the more enthusiasm I put in the more reward I got out and I liked myself more for making the effort. It helped a lot that I changed my situation to a school where the teachers were slightly less dull and uneducated and the children slightly less vile. Deliberately changing my situation was not an act of bad faith but a way of taking possession of my broader being-in-situation. Bad faith is moaning about your circumstances but doing nothing to change them. A teacher in bad faith, or a waiter, or a bus driver, or a soldier, or a sales executive, all resist embracing their being-in-situation. Being-in-situation is a vital feature of being authentic and is central to the project of becoming an existentialist. We will revisit the existentialist idea of being-in-situation in the next chapter.

Homosexuality, sincerity and transcendence

Sartre develops the account of bad faith he gives in *Being and Nothingness* with the famous example of the homosexual. A character that closely resembles the homosexual Sartre describes in *Being and Nothingness* is Daniel Sereno, one of the main characters in a trilogy of novels Sartre wrote called *Roads to Freedom*. Sartre's homosexual does not deny his sexual desires and activities. Instead, he denies that homosexuality is the *meaning* of his conduct. Rather than take responsibility for his gay conduct he chooses to characterize it as a series of aberrations, as mere eccentricity, as the result of curiosity rather than the result of a deep-seated tendency and so on.

He believes a homosexual is not a homosexual as a chair is a chair. This belief is justified in so far as a person is never what he is but only what he aims at being through his choices. The homosexual is quite right that he is not a homosexual-*thing*, but in so far as he has adopted conduct defined as the conduct of a homosexual, he is a homosexual. That he is not a homosexual in the sense that a chair is a chair does not imply that he is not a homosexual in the sense that a chair is not a table. Sartre argues that the homosexual 'plays on the word *being*' (*Being and Nothingness*, p. 87). He slyly interprets 'not being what he *is*', as 'not being what he is not'.

The homosexual attempts to deny altogether that there are various facts about him and that certain meanings can be correctly attached to his behaviour. He attempts to deny altogether that he is his facticity. The truth, however, is that he *is* forever his facticity in the sense of *having been it*, in the sense of *was*. That is, his facticity is his past and because it is *his* past and nobody else's he is forever responsible for it. In other words, though he is not his facticity in the mode of being it, he is his facticity in so far as it is a past that he continually affirms as his by having always to transcend it towards the future. He assumes in bad faith that he is a pure transcendence, that his facticity, his past, has vanished into the absolute nothingness of a generalized past that has nothing whatsoever to do with him. In truth, far from being a pure transcendence, he is and must be the transcendence *of* his facticity. In his project of bad faith the homosexual attempts to force a rift between his facticity and his transcendence when in truth they are locked together as tight as his past and his future.

The homosexual has a friend, a champion of sincerity, who urges him to be sincere, to come out of the proverbial closet and admit that he is gay. In doing so, he urges him to consider himself as just a facticity, as a homosexual-*thing*. In urging the homosexual to consider himself as just a facticity the champion of sincerity aims to stereotype him as *just* a homosexual. Of course, the homosexual is a homosexual, the term 'homosexual' describes him correctly, but he is not *just* a homosexual. It is worth repeating, he is not just a facticity but the transcendence *of* a facticity. The champion of sincerity wants the homosexual to apply the label 'homosexual' to himself. His motive in seeking to stereotype the homosexual and render him two-dimensional is to deny him the dimension of freedom that makes him an individual; it is to transcend him and reduce him to a transcendence-transcended. Once again we discover the struggle for transcendence, the inevitable conflict, that existentialist philosophers argue is at the heart of all human relationships.

Ordinarily, sincerity is admired as a form of honesty or good faith. Sartre, however, in his usual, radical way, exposes sincerity as a form of bad faith. If the homosexual took his friend's advice to be sincere and admitted he was gay, if he declared, 'I am what I am,' he would not overcome his bad faith. He would simply exchange the bad faith of considering himself a pure transcendence for the bad faith of considering himself a pure facticity. To declare, 'I am what I am,' is to assert the fallacy that I am a fixed entity while evading the existential truth that I am an ambiguous and indeterminate being who must continually create myself through choice and action. In short, it is to declare myself a facticity when in reality I am the transcendence *of* my facticity – this is bad faith.

The form of sincerity identified so far is relatively unsophisticated. Sartre also identifies a more sophisticated and devious form of sincerity. This more sophisticated and devious form of sincerity still involves a person declaring, 'I am what I am,' but here his aim is not to be a thing, not to *be* what he is, but to distance himself from what he is by the very act of declaring what he is. In declaring himself to be a thing he aims to become the person who declares he is a thing rather than the thing he declares himself to be. Cunningly, he insists he is as a thing in order to escape being that thing, in order to become the person who contemplates from a distance the thing he has ceased to be.

'I am so lazy' admits Fred, instantly becoming the one who admits to being lazy rather than the one who is *responsible* for being lazy. Unlike a person who adopts the simpler form of sincerity, Fred does not aim to be his facticity by denying his transcendence, he aims to be a pure transcendence divorced from his facticity. The classic example of this more sophisticated form of sincerity is *confession*.

The person who confesses a sin renders his sin into an object for his contemplation that exists only because he contemplates it and ceases to exist when he ceases contemplating it. Believing himself to be a pure transcendence he believes he is free to move on from his sin and abandon it to the past, to the shadows of the confession box, as a disarmed sin that is neither his possession nor his responsibility. Confession that aims at absolution is bad faith.

Some religious groups have made enormous use of this form of bad faith down through the centuries. They offer personalized confession and forgiveness services as a cure for the disease of guilt they spread around for free. It is a brilliant marketing strategy that never goes out of fashion and has paid for a wealth of fancy buildings and bric-a-brac.

To return to the homosexual for a moment, what should he do to avoid being in bad faith and to aspire to authenticity? How should he behave, what new attitude should he adopt? Clearly, he is in bad faith if he denies that homosexuality is the meaning of his conduct. He is equally in bad faith if he insists he is not responsible for his conduct because he *is* a homosexual, a homosexual-*thing*; as though having a certain sexual preference *forces* him to do the things he does. And he is still in bad faith if he confesses that he 'has been' a homosexual as a cunning way of aspiring to no longer be a homosexual. As with the flirt, the homosexual's path out of bad faith is not in fact a complicated one, although he may find it very difficult on a personal and social level to bring himself to take that path. He has to accept that he is a homosexual, not by labelling himself a homosexual-*thing*, but by accepting that his conduct characterizes him as homosexual and not as bisexual or heterosexual or any other kind of sexual. Most importantly, he has to accept that he *chooses* his conduct. He could have chosen to behave differently but he didn't. He is responsible for his conduct and to be authentic he has to *take responsibility* for his conduct. He has to accept that it is a part of himself and always will be. He has to own it.

Arguably, the very deep problem that Sartre's homosexual has is that he doesn't want to be the homosexual he nonetheless chooses to be through his actions. This is almost certainly true of Sartre's homosexual character, Daniel Sereno. Daniel is, as the Americans say, *conflicted*, but if you want to know more about him you'll have to read the novels. To overcome his bad faith Sartre's homosexual would have to take the emotionally difficult step of wanting to be the homosexual his desires and his chosen conduct make him. He has to stop regretting his homosexuality and start affirming it. Part of being a true existentialist is wanting to be what we make ourselves be by the way we choose to act, as opposed to making excuses for the way we act and regretting it. There is a close link between authenticity and refusing to regret which I'll look at in the next chapter.

The homosexual might well need help to achieve such a radical and life changing shift in his attitude. Not from a champion of sincerity who just wants to belittle him by getting him to label himself, but from a true friend, or even an existential counsellor! Yes, there are such creatures as existential counsellors. They practise a method called *existential psychoanalysis* invented by Sartre and developed by the psychiatrist R. D. Laing. Existentialists are a hard-nosed bunch of realists but this doesn't mean they lack compassion or a real interest in using their insights into the human condition to help people *help themselves* get over their hang-ups and start living more honest, positive and less remorse-ridden lives.

In a way, this book is an exercise in existential counselling, if only because it offers advice – that is, counsel – on how to be an existentialist. This doesn't mean you have to read it on a leather couch while paying £50 per hour to a nodding dog, although any donations would be gratefully received. Existential counselling is the focus of the final chapter.

Wilful ignorance

In a book called *Truth and Existence* that he wrote a few years after *Being and Nothingness* Sartre returned once again to the subject of bad faith. In this work he explores the strategies of evasion and self-distraction people employ to avoid the truth and remain ignorant of their real situation, arguing that at heart bad faith is wilful ignorance that aims at the avoidance of responsibility. Ignorance, Sartre notes, is not a lack of knowing. In fact, it is a type of knowledge. To choose to ignore reality is to confirm that it is knowable. Sartre says, 'Ignorance itself as a project is a mode of knowledge since, if I want to ignore Being, it is because I affirm that it is knowable' (*Truth and Existence*, p. 33). Ignorance is motivated by fear and anxiety that knowledge of stark reality is always possible, always lurking. In Sartre's view, as in Nietzsche's, to know the truth, to know the way things are and to see life for what it is, does not require great intelligence but rather honesty and courage in face of reality.

To help explain his theory about bad faith and wilful ignorance Sartre takes the example of a woman with tuberculosis. The woman refuses to acknowledge that she has TB despite having all the symptoms – fatigue, weight loss, night sweats, chest pains, coughing up blood. She views each symptom in isolation, refusing to recognize their collective meaning. She engrosses herself in activities that do not afford her time to visit the doctor, activities that distract her from making the choices required by her situation. Her symptoms place her at the threshold of new knowledge, but she chooses ignorance because she does not want the responsibility of dealing with her TB, of seeking a cure for it and so on, that new knowledge would call for. In her refusal to face her situation, in her self-distraction and her evasion of responsibility, she is similar to Sartre's flirt.

For Sartre, to dispense with wilful ignorance and irresponsibility and instead to courageously affirm the existential truths of the human condition – abandonment in a Godless universe, freedom, responsibility, mortality and so on – is to overcome bad faith in favour of authenticity.

What comes over very strongly in Sartre's fictional writings particularly, his stories, novels and plays, is that people in bad faith 'don't know they're born', or rather, people who 'don't know they're born' are in bad faith. Sartre thinks that there is a widespread tendency among people to avoid confronting what life is really all about, a desperate and sometimes quite violent effort to ignore the hard existential truths of the human condition. One of the hard existential truths that people strive to ignore and deny in the very way they live their lives is what Sartre and other philosophers call *contingency*. A lot can be learnt about bad faith, about a great deal of human behaviour generally, by examining contingency and humankind's various inauthentic reactions to it. So, what is contingency?

Contingency, nausea and the Existential
Alka-Seltzer of bad faith

Contingency is the state of being contingent, unnecessary, accidental. Whatever is contingent is not necessary, it need not be or be so. Sartre identifies contingency as a fundamental feature of the universe, a basic fact of existence as a whole, and he explores the phenomenon in detail, especially in his most famous novel, *Nausea*, a work he nicknamed his 'factum on contingency' while he was writing it; 'factum' being a term he adopted to describe any form of ruthless analysis.

Although in Sartre's opinion existence as such is uncreated and not dependent on anything else for its existence, it is not necessary. It is not the case that it cannot not be, there are no laws of logic or physics or anything else dictating that it must be. It *is*, but it is unnecessary and in being unnecessary it is contingent. For Sartre, existence is contingent in the sense of being absurdly superfluous. It is a grotesque cosmic accident that need not exist but does; a de trop existence that exists for no reason and for no purpose.

Human consciousness is capable of a sickening and terrifying awareness of being submerged in an existence that is absurd, pointless, superfluous and contingent. Sartre calls this sickening and terrifying awareness 'the Nausea' – hence the title of his greatest masterpiece. Human consciousness is, so to speak, even more contingent than the contingent existence of the world, because in having no being of its own it exists only as a *relation* to contingency, as a mere reflection of something gratuitous. For a person to suffer the nausea is for him to experience a ghastly state of naked, superfluous existence that not only surrounds him but is him; his mind and his body.

In the words of Antoine Roquentin, the central character of *Nausea*, 'Things are bad! Things are very bad: I've got it, that filthy thing, the Nausea. And this time it's new: it caught me in a café. Until now cafés were my only refuge because they are full of people and well lighted' (*Nausea*, pp. 32–33). In *Side Effects*, a collection of short stories, existentialism's resident comedian, Woody Allen, recommends Existential Alka-Seltzer, an enormous pill the size of an automobile hub-cap, as a cure for the existential nausea induced by an over-awareness of the contingency of cafés, parks, streets, buses, people and life generally. It is also helpful after eating Mexican food says Allen.

Human society, most human endeavour, constantly aims to suppress contingency by imposing meanings and purposes on the world. This is achieved largely by naming and categorizing things. In naming something people believe they have made sense of it, ascribed meaning to it, grasped its essential essence, removed the contingency of its raw, nameless existence. We all do it. We see an unusual insect in the garden. We look it up in *Collins Complete Guide to Wildlife* and find out its common and Latin names and feel satisfied that we now know what it is, that we have understood it and put it in its place. But does this naming ritual really make the insect less weird, less of a strange cosmic accident?

The truth, according to existentialist philosophers, is that things only have meaning and purpose relative to other things and the whole lot only has the relative meaning and purpose that our ultimately pointless activities give it. Seen for what they are in themselves, apart from the instrumental systems that give them their function or the framework of meanings that seem to explain and justify them, objects are incomprehensible, peculiar, strange, even disturbing in their contingency. Contingency for Sartre is mysterious and to be aware of contingency is to be aware of the unfathomable mystery of being.

If you think existentialism and mysticism have nothing in common, Zen think again. The philosopher Schopenhauer, who had a huge influence on Nietzsche and existentialism generally, was himself heavily influenced by Buddhism. There are certainly many similarities between the existentialist and the Buddhist approaches to life. It would require another book to explore them adequately so I can only suggest you read some of the many excellent works already written on the subject, such as *Lack and Transcendence: The Problem of Death and Life in Psychotherapy, Existentialism and Buddhism* by David Loy or *Nothingness and Emptiness: A Buddhist Engagement with the Ontology of Jean-Paul Sartre* by Stephen Laycock. That should keep you busy.

Sartre does not recommend that people should be like Antoine Roquentin in *Nausea*, always dwelling obsessively on contingency, always striving to live under the aspect of eternity in a meaningless and absurd world. That way lies madness. Sartre himself, like most people most of the time, lived and acted in the world of relative meanings and purposes. Like most people most of the time, he kept his sanity and sense of perspective by directing his attentions to the task in hand, to the daily round of 'doing his thing', which for him was mainly hanging out in cafés and writing, often at the same time. He wasn't big on retail therapy or DIY and I guess never mowed a lawn or washed a car in his entire life, but he was always busy.

He believed, nonetheless, that an occasional or background aware-ness of contingency is vital if a person is to achieve any degree of authen-ticity and avoid living a lie. Sartre's philosophy is characterized by an abiding hatred and distrust of people, usually middle-class (bourgeois) people, who seem totally unaware of life's contingency; people who once glimpsed life's contingency and were terrified by it and are now on the run from it. The fundamental project of these people is to evade their own contingency and that of the world by acting in bad faith.

The world, they tell themselves in bad faith, is not contingent but created with humankind as its centrepiece. They assume that they have an immortal essence, that their existence is inevitable, that they exist by some divine decree rather than by accident. They believe the moral and social values they subscribe to are objective, absolute and unquestiona-ble. They believe that society is rooted in these absolute values and that the way things are in society constitutes the only possible reality. All they have to do to claim their absolute right to be respected by others and to have the respect of others sustain the illusion of their necessity is to dutifully fulfil the role prescribed to them by society and identify themselves totally with that role. They learn to see themselves only as others see them and avoid thinking about themselves in any kind of philosophical way. Dwelling on the strangeness and contingency of their existence is strictly off limits. As far as possible, they avoid thinking about anything at all, except on the most mundane and clichéd level. You have probably met these people. You can recognize them by their conversation. When you talk with them you feel you are following a script that permits the listing of mundane facts and forbids all discussion, analysis, introspection and flights of imagination.

The existentialist philosopher, Kierkegaard, writes about people who suffer from what he calls 'objective madness'. People with objective madness do not really exist because they have completely lost themselves to objectivity by preoccupying themselves with facts: they even consider themselves to be just another fact. Kierkegaard contrasts 'objective madness' with 'subjective madness', what is commonly understood as madness. For Kierkegaard, the person who suffers from objective madness is far less human, has far less soul, than a person who suffers from subjective madness. The subjective madman is all too human, his madness reveals his living soul.

A good example of a subjective madman is Don Quixote. A good example of an objective madwoman is former British Prime Minister, Margaret Thatcher, although most politicians would fit the bill. In a sense, Don Quixote is far more real as a fictional character than Thatcher is as a factual character. Kierkegaard writes, 'One shrinks from looking into the eyes of a madman [with subjective madness] lest one be compelled to plumb there the depths of his delirium; but one dares not look at a madman [with objective madness] at all, from fear of discovering that he has eyes of glass and hair made from carpet rags; that he is, in short, an artificial product' (*Concluding Unscientific Postscript*, p. 175).

Moustaches and *salauds*

In Sartre's writing people with what Kierkegaard calls 'objective madness' very often grow a moustache. For Sartre, the moustache becomes the emblem of unthinking men with no inner life. A man can not see his own moustache, at least to the extent that others see it, so a moustache exists primarily for others and a man with a moustache is a man who has undertaken to exist for others rather than for himself. In so far as it is typical of the bourgeois to strive to *be* his social role, the moustache, for Sartre, becomes the emblem of the shallow, self-satisfied, respectable, reactionary middle-class gentleman. 'The fine gentleman exists Legion of Honour, exists moustache, that's all; how happy one must be to be nothing more than a Legion of Honour and a moustache and nobody sees the rest, he sees the two pointed ends of moustache on both sides of the nose; I do not think therefore I am a moustache' (*Nausea*, p. 147).

Maybe Sartre is too hard on people with moustaches. Perhaps he is jealous because he couldn't grow a big macho tache himself. I'm sure history is full of authentic characters and true existentialists with big taches. I mean, Nietzsche had a huge one, moustache that is. Nonetheless, if you want to be an existentialist and you have a moustache you need to think very hard about why you have it, why you shave your whole face except that bit between your mouth and nose. (I'm not sure where Sartre stood on beards.)

I'm certainly not going to advise you to shave off your tache. If becoming an existentialist was as easy as following petty rules about the presence or absence of facial hair then there would be millions of existentialists trying to take over the world rather than just a near-extinct handful hiding out in cheap cafés and dingy garrets. Once again, being an existentialist is not so much about what you do, as your attitude to what you do. As always, the *choice* is yours.

The most profound denial of contingency, the most extreme bad faith, is achieved by people Sartre calls *salauds* – French for swine or bastards. Sartre details the personal development of a typical salaud in a brilliant short story he wrote called *The Childhood of a Leader*. A *salaud* is as far from a true existentialist as you can get.

The story traces the emotional, psychological, social, sexual and moral development of a privileged bourgeois, Lucien Fleurier, from

infancy to adulthood. Lucien's childhood and adolescence are characterized by his quest to understand who he is, to find and define himself, to give himself a solidity and reality that replaces the vagueness
and insubstantiality he usually feels. In feeling indeterminate and contingent he recognizes the existential truth that there is nothing that he
is in the manner of being it. Like everyone else he must play at being
what he is because he cannot simply *be* what he is. Lucien, however,
like many people, does not like this sense of his own contingency, it
makes him uncomfortable and anxious. He tries various strategies to
overcome it as he grows, eventually choosing to think and act in profound bad faith, creating and forcing himself to believe in the illusion
of his own necessity and determinacy.

Lucien blames a homosexual encounter he has in his teens on the
ideas of Sigmund Freud, who happens to be Jewish. Raised in an anti-
Semitic environment it is easy for Lucien to convince himself that the
dangerous, perverted, Jewish ideas of Freud temporarily corrupted his
moral health and led him to his gay fling. He adopts anti-Semitism as a
distraction from his homosexual desires. What he really fears and hates
are his desires, but to hate them would be to recognize that he has
them, so he hates Jews instead.

He embraces the security and respectability of his wealthy family,
looking forward to the day when he will inherit Daddy's factory and be
respected by his workers. He adopts Daddy's positive view of capital-
ism, his nationalism and above all his anti-Semitism. He joins the French
Fascist movement and helps to beat up an immigrant in a racially motivated attack. Membership of this aggressive, macho, anti-intellectual
tribe makes him feel strong and proud and gives him a sense of belong-
ing. He had formerly searched for his *personal* identity, but now he is
happy to take on an identity granted and confirmed by the group.

In fiercely despising Jews, his badge of honour among his fellow
Fascists, he not only finds a scapegoat for his past actions, he sees him-
self as important and substantial in comparison to people he despises.
He prides himself that he is not a member of a despised race, but

a Frenchman with a good French name and respectable ancestry. His anti-Semitism, unreasonable and unfounded though it is, transforms him into a man of conviction. His convictions define him and give him solidity; they demand the respect of others.

The transformation in Lucien's self-image, the construction of his false object-self, is finally completed when, dissatisfied with his pretty, childish face, he decides to grow a moustache. Lucien's slide into chronic, cowardly, morally repugnant bad faith is complete. He has become an absolute *salaud*, a total swine. He has persuaded himself that his existence is not accidental but essential and that he has sacred *rights* granted by God and his nation, such as the right to have unquestionable opinions and prejudices and the right to have his necessary existence confirmed by the respect of others, especially his social inferiors.

Sartre's contempt for *salauds* reaches its height in *Nausea* when he has the novel's central character, Antoine Roquentin, visit a museum to look at the ostentatious portraits of the respectable, dutiful, now dead elders of Bouville – a town loosely based on the port of Le Havre where Sartre lived for several years. Antoine realizes that these portraits are a vain, arrogant, absurd lie. They portray the elders as taller, grander, wealthier, more significant, more substantial and infinitely less contingent than they ever were in real life. In having themselves portrayed in this fashion the elders were attempting to convince themselves and others of their necessity and indispensability; that they had a God given place in the universe and society, and above all that they had *rights*. In *Sartre: Romantic Rationalist*, Iris Murdoch writes, 'Their faces are *éclatant de droit* – blazing with right. Their lives had a real *given* meaning, or so they imagined; and here they are, with all that added sense of necessity with which the painter's thought can endow them' (*Sartre: Romantic Rationalist*, p. 12).

Though dead, there is a sense in which the elders are still trying to convince the world of their superiority and their entitlements. The portraits give the lie that these people have not really died but merely transcended to an even higher, even more respectable social class. The class of the super-bourgeoisie. They are like the middle-class people in the Monty Python film *The Meaning of Life* who die of food poisoning after eating salmon mouse. When the Grim Reaper claims them they drive to middle-class heaven in a Volvo, a Rover and a Porsche. One couple per car. They don't think to car-share on their final journey. Middle-class heaven, incidentally, is a five star hotel with a large entertainments lounge where it is always Christmas.

The *salauds* and the profound bad faith that characterizes them is well summed up in *Nausea* in Sartre's (Antoine's) mocking account of Jean Pacôme, one of Bouville's most eminent deceased citizens:

> I hadn't any right to exist. I had appeared by chance, I existed like a stone, a plant, a microbe. . . . But for this handsome, impeccable man, now dead, for Jean Pacôme, the son of the Pacôme of the Government of National Defence, it had been an entirely different matter: the beating of his heart and the dull rumblings of his organs reached him in the form of pure and instantaneous little rights. For sixty years, without a moments failing, he had made use of his right to live. These magnificent grey eyes had never been clouded by the slightest doubt. Nor had Pacôme ever made a mistake. (*Nausea*, p. 124)

As a person who constantly recognizes that life has no meaning or purpose, Sartre is fascinated by the lies and bad faith by which *salauds* seek to give their lives meaning and purpose. His alter-ego, Antoine, feels nothing but contempt for the idiotic hat raising and idle chatter people indulge in to pass the time on a Sunday morning along the exclusive rue Tournebride. 'I see hats, a sea of hats. Most of them are black and hard. Now and then you see one fly off at the end of an arm, revealing the soft gleam of a skull; then, after a few moments of clumsy flight, it settles again . . . "Good morning, Monsieur. Good morning, my dear sir, how are you keeping? Do put your hat on again, Monsieur, you'll catch cold. Thank you, Madame, it isn't very warm, is it?"' (*Nausea*, pp. 67–68).

Of course, if life is an utterly meaningless and pointless cosmic accident then hat raising rituals and idle chitchat are no more absurd than anything else people do and are as good a way as any to pass the time between a pointless birth and a meaningless death.

Sartre, largely as a reaction to his own bourgeois upbringing, consistently despises the bad faith that so characterizes the middle classes, but what, really, is so wrong with bad faith on a mundane level? Bad faith provides coping strategies, it is a guard rail against the kind of anxiety that makes Antoine's life so wretched. Even Nietzsche, the great champion of authenticity, recognizes in *Beyond Good and Evil*, 'the *narrowing of perspective*, and thus in a certain sense stupidity, as a condition of life and growth' (*Beyond Good and Evil*, 188, p. 112).

Sartre would definitely reply to the question, 'What is wrong with bad faith?', by saying that it is unthinking, lazy and life denying, that it oppresses the true, free human spirit, that it is a banal evil central to the hypocrisy and irresponsibility that causes so much trouble, strife and suffering in the world. History, he would say, is characterized by injustice and violence, very often the injustice and violence of ordinary folk who acted in profound bad faith when they made those all too familiar excuses, 'I was only doing my job,' 'I was only following orders,' 'They made me do it,' 'I couldn't help it.'

***

I have now outlined the attitudes and behaviours you must *avoid* if you want to be a true existentialist. It is now time that we focused on what you actually have to *do* in a positive sense to be a true existentialist, apart from knowing about existentialism and roughly subscribing to it. It is surely no longer a secret, as I've more than hinted at it several times already, that being a true existentialist has a great deal to do with being authentic, or more precisely, with behaving authentically. So, without much further ado I offer you the final chapter of this peculiar self-help guide that I hope will at least point you in the general direction of authentic existence.

It's one thing to read and write about authentic existence, another far greater thing to achieve it, and I make no claims to having achieved it, although I believe I've got close to it a few times in my life so far.

I am no Guru, which is just as well, as existentialism and being an existentialist are definitely not about *following* people, especially not blindly. Existentialism isn't a religion, that much I do know. Of course, if you want to send me money like people do to those Gurus in India then please go ahead. Think of me, this little book, more as a signpost; a rickety signpost languishing on a grassy verge at a quiet crossroads somewhere in England; a signpost that for some reason is pointing the way to Alpha Centauri. Reach for the stars!

4 How to Be Authentic

If we have learnt anything so far about authenticity it is that it is the opposite of bad faith. Bad faith is inauthenticity. We have also learnt that authenticity is distinct from sincerity. Sincerity is a form of bad faith. Sartre's examples of people in bad faith reveal that the most blatant feature of inauthenticity is *the attempt to evade responsibility*. Sartre's flirt attempts to evade responsibility for her present situation while Sartre's homosexual attempts to evade responsibility for his past deeds. As for people who are sincere in the way advocated by the champion of sincerity, they admit to being something as a sneaky way of dumping responsibility for it.

Inauthentic people sustain particular projects of avoiding responsibility for their present situation or their past deeds by refusing in bad faith to admit that they are responsible. More specifically, they refuse to admit the inability of the self to coincide with itself as a facticity or as a pure transcendence, and they refuse to admit the unlimited or near unlimited freedom of the self and what this freedom implies. They refuse to recognize that a person must always choose what he is because he is unable simply to *be* what he is. As we know, a person cannot not choose his responses to his situation, and because his responses to his situation are chosen, he is responsible for his choices. Even if he chooses to do nothing that is still a choice he is responsible for.

Authenticity and getting real

Inauthenticity is the denial of the fundamental existential truth that we are free and responsible, whereas authenticity, as the antithesis of inauthenticity, is the acceptance or affirmation of this fundamental existential truth. Authenticity involves a person confronting reality and facing up to the hard truth that he is at all times a free being who will never obtain coincidence with himself. Whereas the inauthentic person tries to avoid recognizing that this is the fundamental truth of his life, the authentic person not only recognizes it, he strives to come to terms with it and even to treat it as a source of values. The authentic person responds fully to the appeal to *get real* that pervades existentialism. In his *War Diaries* Sartre writes that authenticity 'consists in adopting human reality as one's own' (*War Diaries*, p. 113). That is, authenticity consists in embracing human reality for what it is and living in accordance with it rather than pretending it is something else: a nice fairytale reality where dreams come true without effort, where debts don't have to be paid back, where knights in shining armour ride to the rescue and we all live happily ever after.

As a radical conversion that involves a person *affirming* what in fact he has always been – a free and responsible being lacking coincidence with himself – adopting human reality as his own involves a radical shift in a person's attitude towards himself and his unavoidable *situatedness*. Instead of exercising his freedom in order to deny his freedom, instead of acting in bad faith choosing not to choose, the authentic person *assumes* his freedom and acknowledges it in a positive way.

Assuming freedom involves a person assuming total responsibility for himself in whatever situation he finds himself. It involves accepting without complaint that this and no other is his situation; that this situation is the facticity in terms of which he must now choose himself. If he is not imprisoned he can, of course, reject his situation by running away, and often beating a hasty retreat is a wise option, but this still involves a choice. A choice that gives rise to new situations and to new demands to choose. With the exception of suicide – the toughest choice of all – it is not possible to run away from being situated altogether, and every situation is a demand to choose. Above all, assuming his freedom involves realizing that because he is nothing in the manner of being it he is nothing but the choices he makes in his situation.

Being-in-situation

In his *War Diaries* Sartre writes about his inauthentic friend Paul who is a soldier. Paul is not a soldier in the manner of being a soldier-*thing*, but as he fights in an army 'soldier' is the meaning of Paul's conduct. Paul says, 'Me, a soldier? I consider myself a civilian in military disguise' (*War Diaries*, p. 112). This declaration reveals Paul is not taking responsibility for his choices. Sartre says, 'He thus stubbornly continues to *flee* what he's *making of himself*' (*War Diaries*, p. 112). Paul flees what he is making of himself – a soldier – towards the non-existent civilian he mistakenly fancies himself to be.

Paul is an example of what Sartre calls a 'buffeted consciousness' (*War Diaries*, p. 112). He has not accepted his 'being-in-situation' (*War Diaries*, p. 54). In denying that he is only ever his response to his facticity Paul pleads the excuse of his facticity. He chooses to see himself as a facticity, as a given entity buffeted along by circumstances. It is in ceasing to be like Paul and accepting his being-in-situation that a person ceases to be a buffeted consciousness, gets a grip on himself and becomes authentic. The following passage from Sartre's *War Diaries* sums up better than anything else he ever wrote what he thinks authenticity involves:

> To be authentic is to realise fully one's being-in-situation, whatever this situation may happen to be: with a profound awareness that, through the authentic realisation of the being-in-situation, one brings to full existence the situation on the one hand and human reality on the other. This presupposes a patient

study of what the situation requires, and then a way of throwing oneself into
it and determining oneself to 'be-for' this situation. (*War Diaries*, p. 54)

Imagine an alternative reality where Paul is authentic. How does
authentic Paul behave? Authentic Paul understands that his present
situation requires him to play to the full the role of a soldier. This doesn't
mean he *pretends* to be a soldier. Pretending to be a soldier is what
inauthentic Paul does by considering himself to be a civilian in military
disguise. In playing at being a soldier to the full, authentic Paul aims at
being a soldier all the way, making himself 'be-for' the military situation and absorbing himself in that situation. He does not believe he is a
soldier in the manner of being one, but neither does he disbelieve he is
a soldier in the sense of believing he is really something other than a
soldier; something other than his current role. The same can be said for
him as was said earlier for Sartre's waiter: He absorbs himself in his *performance* so much that he does not reflect on the fact he is performing.
He has become his performance and his attitude towards himself
involves a suspension of disbelief.

Inauthentic Paul is full of excuses. By declaring that he is not really a
soldier but a civilian in disguise he wants to be excused responsibility
for the situation he is in and his actions in that situation. But if a person
wants to be authentic he has to recognize that there are no excuses for
his actions; and even if excuses are possible for some of his actions,
because people are not responsible for absolutely everything they do,
he is not going to make any excuses. To be authentic a person must
resist by an act of will any desire for excuses. Sartre says, 'Of course, it's
a question not just of *recognising* that one has no excuse, but also of
willing it' (*War Diaries*, p. 113). Maybe excuses can sometimes be justified, maybe they can never be justified, existentialist philosophers are
divided on the matter. What matters, if you want to obtain the holy
grail of authenticity, is that you have to totally quit making excuses like
a reformed alcoholic has to totally quit drinking alcohol.

Authentic Paul not only recognizes that in his current situation there
are no excuses not to play at being a soldier, he does not want there to

be any excuses. To be truly authentic, Paul must fully realise his being-in-situation without regret. If authentic Paul does not want to be where he is he will leave without regret and face the consequences of desertion without regret. If he stays, he will assume responsibility for his staying and throw himself into the spirit of things. Sartre, as he recounts in his *War Diaries*, attempted to do just this. Rather than complain that he was really a sophisticated Parisian intellectual forced by circumstances to join an army unit exiled to the arse end of nowhere, he attempted to make the most of his situation and dedicate himself without remorse to his current role of 'soldier' – albeit a soldier with few duties who was often at liberty to read and write for sixteen hours a day. Sartre had so much time on his hands during the 'phoney war' that preceded the German invasion of France in 1940 that he is supposed to have written a million words in eight months.

The idea that living authentically involves living without regret is central to Nietzsche's view of authenticity. We'll look at what Nietzsche has to say shortly.

Freedom as a value

Authenticity involves a person coming to terms with the fact that he will never be at one with himself, that he will never become a kind of *thing* that no longer has to choose what it is. Surprisingly though, authenticity does not involve a person abandoning the desire for oneness, substantiality and foundation. The desire to have a foundation, to be its own foundation, is fundamental to the human will so it can never abandon this desire. Sartre says, 'The first value and first object of will is: to be its own foundation. This mustn't be understood as an empty psychological desire, but as the transcendental structure of human reality' (*War Diaries*, p. 110). Any attempt to abandon altogether the desire for foundation collapses into a project of *nihilism*. In trying to escape his desire for foundation a person can only aim at being nothing at all.

Far from being in good faith, a nihilistic person who tells himself that he is in fact nothing, is actually in bad faith. His bad faith consists in his false belief that he is his own nothingness in the manner of being it, a nothingness-in-itself, when in fact his nothingness consists in his being nothing but a relationship to the world he is conscious of. For a person to believe that deep down he is a nothingness-in-itself is equivalent to believing that deep down he is something fixed and determined. As both attitudes involve considering himself to be a self-identical being that is what it is without having to choose what it is, both attitudes are equally in bad faith.

In her book, *The Ethics of Ambiguity*, Simone de Beauvoir compares the nihilist who wants to be nothing with the serious person who seeks to annihilate his subjectivity by treating himself as an object entirely defined by social norms and conventions.

> The failure of the serious sometimes brings about a radical disorder. Conscious of being unable to be anything, man then decides to be nothing. We shall call this attitude nihilistic. The nihilist is close to the spirit of seriousness, for instead of realising his negativity as a living movement, he conceives his annihilation in a substantial way. He wants to *be* nothing, and this nothing that he dreams of is still another sort of being. (*The Ethics of Ambiguity*, p. 52)

So, the project of authenticity is still motivated by the search for substantiality and foundation, but it differs crucially from bad faith in that, as Sartre says, 'it suppresses that which, in the search, is flight' (*War Diaries*, p. 112). What does he mean?

What Sartre means is that the authentic person does not aim at oneness, foundation, substantiality, by means of a futile flight from his freedom. Instead, he aims at substantiality by continually founding himself upon the affirmation and assertion of his freedom. He takes the affirmation and assertion of his freedom as his basic principle or ultimate value. He seeks to identify himself with his inalienable freedom rather than flee his inalienable freedom in the vain hope of becoming a fixed *thing*.

The project of authenticity is actually more successful at achieving a kind of substantiality than the project of inauthenticity because the project of authenticity reconciles a person to what he really is, an essentially free being, whereas the project of inauthenticity is only ever a flight from what a person really is towards an unachievable identity with the world of objects. In fleeing freedom a person does not establish a foundation, but in assuming his freedom he establishes freedom itself as a foundation. In assuming his freedom he 'becomes' what he is – free – rather than failing to become what he can never be – unfree. To put it another way, the desire for constancy can only be satisfied by embracing freedom because freedom is the only thing about a person that is constant. Sartre says, 'Thus authenticity is a value but not primary. It gives itself as a means to arrive at substantiality' (*War Diaries*, p. 112).

It is important to note that the form of substantiality arrived at through authenticity is not a fixed state. As said, it is logically impossible for consciousness to achieve a fixed state and all attempts to do so involve bad faith. The substantiality achieved through authenticity is not achieved by consciousness once and for all, it is a substantiality that has to *be* continually perpetuated and re-assumed. A person cannot simply be authentic, he *has to be* authentic. That is, he has to constantly strive to be authentic without ever being able to become an authentic-*thing*. If a person ever thinks he *is* authentic in the same way that a rock *is* a rock, he is no longer authentic and has actually slid back into bad faith. Authenticity is not a permanent foundation that a person chooses to establish at a particular time once and for all, but rather what existentialist philosophers call a *metastable foundation* that a person must constantly maintain by constantly choosing authentic responses to his situation.

The problem of *being* authentic

This book is called *How to Be an Existentialist*, but only now is it becoming clear that it is not actually possible to *be* a true existentialist, to *be* authentic. I almost feel like apologizing for misleading people, but I think maybe the explanation would not have made complete sense until now. You can never just be converted into a true existentialist –

read the book, pass the exam, get the certificate. An Olympic champion *is* an Olympic champion for four years even if he never runs another race, but an authentic person must run the race of authenticity all the time. He is only authentic when he *behaves* authentically and he can never look to his laurels or even think that he is authentic. To think he is authentic is to think he is an authentic-*thing*, and as we've seen, for a person to think he is any kind of thing is bad faith.

The fact that even thinking 'I am authentic' prevents a person from achieving authenticity seems to be a real problem for anyone who tries to deliberately think his or her way towards authenticity; a real problem for anyone hoping to achieve authenticity as a result of reading this book! The only hope I can see, perhaps, is that when you have finished reading this book you donate it to Oxfam or auction it on ebay and try to forget all about it as you set about behaving authentically. Despite my positive comments elsewhere in this book, I can't get rid of a nagging suspicion that intellectuals have a real problem when it comes to behaving authentically, because it seems to me that a person just can't behave authentically if he thinks he is doing so. There may be a tiny loop hole out of this dilemma which I'll look at shortly, to do with exactly how a person thinks about his authenticity.

Authenticity is not a possession or an essence, it is the way a person chooses to respond to his facticity and the way he chooses himself in response to his facticity. Authenticity is the continuous task of choosing responses that affirm freedom and responsibility rather than responses that signify a flight from freedom and responsibility. The authentic person takes on the task of continually resisting the slide into bad faith that threatens every human project.

I've said that authenticity involves living without regret. If this is so then the following objection regarding the very possibility of authenticity rears its ugly head: Arguably, authenticity is impossible because it is impossible to live without regret. Regret, it seems, is an unavoidable part of the human condition because anyone with the capacity to imagine alternatives can't help wishing, at least occasionally, that he had made a different choice.

A possible reply to this objection is that it does not show authenticity is impossible, simply that it is very difficult to achieve. If a person can come to regret less, as undoubtedly he can by employing various strategies such as anti-depressants, psychotherapy or the study of existentialism, then arguably he has the potential to master himself completely and regret nothing. Maybe he can become like the Duke of Wellington whose no regrets policy was expressed in his famous maxim, 'Never apologise, never explain.'

Maybe the task of complete self-mastery and self-overcoming is too difficult to achieve in one lifetime, particularly for people raised in our culture of excuse and regret. Yet surely it is an heroic ideal worth striving for because it is always better to get real, get a grip and make a stand than it is to be a buffeted consciousness tossed around by everything and everyone. It is better, not least, because a person who constantly strives to confront his situation and overcome it, a person who by this means constantly strives to confront and overcome himself, gains nobility and self-respect. A cowardly person, on the other hand, who dwells on regret, refusing to confront his situation and his being in that situation, knows only his own weakness and sense of defeat; his own lack of nobility and dignity.

Remember nobility and dignity? They are virtues that all but died out sometime during the twentieth century. English gentlemen of the old school appeared to have lots of both. Talentless minor celebrities who appear on reality TV shows totally lack either. Today, nobility is seen only in films about the Roman and Medieval periods and dignity concerns only elderly patients wanting a bed pan. Nobility and dignity need to be reinstated as important virtues, with a lot less emphasis on sympathy and the toleration of failure, negligence and self-neglect. Today, the failure and sloppiness of too many greedy, lazy, irresponsible, wilfully ignorant, other-blaming people who whine that they did their best when they clearly didn't is just too readily excused.

That noble old stalwart, Winston Churchill, once said, 'It's not enough that we do our best; sometimes we have to do what's required.' He recognized that saying 'I did my best' is often a rather pathetic excuse, a display of bad faith, because it's only ever said when the best a person could do wasn't good enough. The logical objection is that a person can't do better than his best if he really did his best, but does a person ever know he really did his best, that he couldn't have done just that tiny bit better? A true existentialist approaches life with the attitude that he can always do better, or at least with the attitude that he only approaches his best if he achieves what he set out to achieve, which is certainly not to fail in doing what is required.

Clearly, this is all extremely unfair on gutsy people who, despite moving heaven and earth and bursting every sinew, are defeated by a truly gifted opponent, impossible odds, circumstances beyond their control or just the bloody weather, but that doesn't matter. The priority here is not to be fair to everyone, to avoid saying what is harsh just in case someone gets offended, it is to identify a good attitude to life; and certainly a good, noble, dignified, existentialist attitude to life is to always avoid saying 'I did my best,' not least because you probably didn't and because you will probably do much better next time. Nobility and dignity are true existentialist virtues.

***

Sartre acknowledges that bad faith threatens every project of the human being. A person has to be almost super human to always avoid sliding into bad faith. A person slides into bad faith the moment he ceases meticulously avoiding the world's endless temptations to slide. Bad faith is so convenient and so seductive that it is very difficult to resist all of the time.

Considering the world's endless temptations to slide into bad faith and the difficulties people face in resisting them, Sartre takes the example of a family man who is called to war (*War Diaries*, pp. 220–221). Prior to his call-up the man was a boring bourgeois who treated his life as though it was on rails with a course dictated by the expectations of his family and his profession. He allowed himself to be what others wanted him to be. The stark realities of war open his eyes and inspire him to put his life into perspective. He assumes his freedom and becomes his own man. Sartre says, 'He's led to *think* about those [past] situations, to make resolutions for the future, and to establish guide-lines for *keeping* authenticity as he moves on to other events' (*War Diaries*, pp. 220–221). He has become a warrior and wishes to remain a warrior even after the war. A man who is ready for anything, a man who takes responsibility for himself and does not make excuses. A strong, silent, noble, dignified type who refuses to compromise himself or to say what others want to hear just because they want to hear it.

Resistance to his noble resolution comes not from within him but from the world around him and from his own past. In Sartre's words, 'Resistance comes, not from residues of inauthenticity which may remain here and there in a badly dusted-off consciousness, but simply from the fact that his previous situations resist the change as *things*' (*War Diaries*, p. 221).

His wife, who he still loves, comes to visit him at the front with all the expectations he has always fulfilled for her in the past. Without any effort or intention he behaves differently towards her simply because he is different. Her expectations, however, present him with the image of his former inauthentic self. This is the real test of his newfound authen-ticity because 'he can't revert to his old errors vis-à-vis that woman without, at a stroke, tumbling headlong into inauthenticity' (*War Dia-ries*, p. 221). His love for his wife means that it is likely he will slide into inauthenticity by conforming to her expectations of him, 'For, presuma-bly, a being who expects the inauthentic of us will freeze us to the mar-row with inauthenticity, by reviving our old love' (*War Diaries*, p. 221).

Sartre goes on to say that such inauthenticity 'is an imposed inau-thenticity, against which it is easy but painful to defend oneself' (*War Diaries*, p. 221). But if imposed inauthenticity is painful to resist then how can it be easy to resist? If it is because of his love for his wife that the man succumbs to imposed inauthenticity, then maybe it is as diffi-cult for him to resist imposed inauthenticity as it is for him to resist loving his wife.

Sartre would reply that it is in fact easy for the man to stop loving his wife and so resist imposed inauthenticity because love is only the choice to be in love. But can any man really *choose* to stop loving his wife? Is Sartre right to insist that emotional states have no momentum of their own or is this, once again, old Sartre taking his radical freedom and choice thesis far too far? I'm going to duck out of answering this complicated question by saying that the answer to it is still a matter of much debate among Sartre nerds.

The difficulties facing a person striving for sustained authentic existence are enormous. In his *War Diaries* Sartre acknowledges his own failure to achieve sustained authentic existence. 'I am not authentic, I have halted on the threshold of the promised lands. But at least I point the way to them and others can go there' (*War Diaries*, p. 62). Sartre does not mention, however, why others should achieve what he, of all people, failed to achieve. If the great champion of authenticity, with his vast will power and his superior mental strength cannot achieve authentic existence, what hope is there for the rest of us?

A quick summary: Authentic existence is a project that has to be continually reassumed. A person is only as authentic as his present act. Even if he has been consistently authentic for a whole week, if he is not authentic right now then he is not authentic. Given the world's endless temptations to bad faith, the difficulties of resisting regret and imposed inauthenticity, the fact that habit and other people's expectations shape a person's life as much as his capacity to choose, it is very difficult for anyone to sustain authenticity for a significant period of time. Most people are probably only capable of achieving authenticity occasionally. Nevertheless, authenticity is an existentialist ideal worth struggling for.

Authenticity and intelligence

The pursuit of authenticity as most existentialist philosophers see it requires a person to be intellectually aware of certain truths of the human condition. To affirm freedom as an ultimate goal, for example, it seems a person must first realize the futility of trying to be at one with himself, of trying to be a *thing* that does not have to make choices.

When existentialist philosophers criticize a person for his inauthenticity – as they are very fond of doing – they do not seem to fully appreciate that the person may simply not realize he is inauthentic. The person may genuinely believe, knowing no better, that it is possible for him to be at one with himself. He is unlikely, of course, to present his belief to himself in such intellectual terms. His belief will more likely take the form of a faith in the possibility of satisfying all his desires and achieving complete fulfilment. Similarly, if a person is not aware of the existential truth that he is only his being-in-situation then inevitably he will believe he is what he has always been rather than what he has suddenly become. He will believe, for example, that he is a civilian in disguise rather than a soldier, if the role of civilian is all he knew prior to his conscription.

Against this kind of criticism existentialist philosophers will insist that it only takes limited intelligence to recognize the existential truths of the human condition. They are not mysterious truths buried in obscure works of philosophy. Everyday life is a hard lesson in the elusiveness of satisfaction, the contingency of existence, the immanence of death and so on. If people do not see these existential truths and the implications of these truths, it is not because they are uninformed, but because they refuse to confront them. It is because they are exercising wilful ignorance motivated by cowardice and sustained by bad faith.

In most cases, it is not because people lack the intelligence that they do not see the existential truths of the human condition, but because they do not want to see them. The fact that they do not want to see them implies, of course, that they have already seen them. Having already seen them and having been made terribly anxious at the sight of them they desperately want to avoid seeing them again. The way they avoid seeing them again is by resorting to bad faith.

There was once a woman whose father died. She was the kind of woman who insisted on being carefree and optimistic so when her friends gave her their condolences she replied that she hoped the same thing never happened to them. But, of course, everyone who doesn't die first suffers their father's death. If this seems an improper thing to say then that is due to the influence of bad faith. Finding hard truths offensive is one of the most common expressions of bad faith. As said, bad faith is wilful ignorance. Bad faith is a coping strategy that helps people avoid overwhelming anguish. If this is so then ironically there is a kind of wisdom in the wilful ignorance of people who lack the courage to confront the hard truths of the human condition. As they say in Yorkshire, it is wise to be 'thick ont' right side'.

If the pursuit of authenticity was necessarily an intellectual project, then only educated people would pursue authenticity, which is certainly not the case. History shows that uneducated people strive to assume their freedom, just as it shows that Heidegger, an expert in the *theory* of existentialism, gave way to the inauthenticity of anti-Semitism and joined Hitler's National Socialist Party.

Although the pursuit of authenticity need not necessarily be an intellectual project, some people are, nevertheless, inspired to pursue authenticity as a direct result of studying existentialism. Studying existentialism highlights existential truths, exposes bad faith and emphasizes the necessity of freedom and responsibility. Studying existentialism can be a process of profound personal enlightenment that influences the very nature of a person's existence in the world.

In an age when philosophy is often regarded simply as an academic subject alongside other academic subjects, the claim that profound personal enlightenment can result from the study of philosophy sounds grandiose. According to the Ancient Greek founders of Western philosophy, however, achieving personal enlightenment is precisely the point of studying philosophy. The trouble with too many philosophy students and teachers is that they think the point of studying philosophy is to get a Philosophy degree and to hell with enlightenment.

For the Ancient Greek philosopher Plato, for example, the purpose of studying philosophy, especially his philosophy, is to achieve knowledge of the fundamental truths that enable a person to distinguish appearance from reality. Like Platonism, although its world-view is very different, existentialism offers enlightenment and a way out of the dark cave of ignorance. In his most famous work, *The Republic*, Plato compares the process of enlightenment to the ascent of a person from a world of shadows within a cave up into the clear light of day.

This is all well and good but the nagging doubt I raised earlier remains: Can a person become authentic as a result of an intellectual process? Sure, studying philosophy can give him all sorts of noble intentions as well as a relatively useful qualification, but doesn't his thinking, 'I am authentic,' immediately spoil whatever authenticity he has attained? As said, a person cannot simply *be* authentic, he has to constantly behave authentically, and thinking he *is* authentic is not behaving authentically. Then again, perhaps my nagging doubt isn't so serious after all. What is really so wrong with a person who is behaving authentically thinking 'I am behaving authentically at the moment'? Does thinking this really make his action inauthentic? Consider a comparative case:–

If, while I'm helping an old lady carry a heavy box up a flight of stairs, I think, 'This is my good deed for the day,' does that suddenly make my deed a selfish act? It is just an idle thought. I was once encouraged to think this idle thought by an old lady who said to me, 'It's your good deed for the day young man.' It seems absurd to suggest the old dear transformed the quality of my action simply by popping this mundane thought into my head. Our attitude to our actions is important and can influence the character of what we do, but we shouldn't always attach too much significance to the casual and arbitrary thoughts that shoot through our minds while we are doing what we do.

Authenticity and other people

Looking back on what has been said so far in this chapter about authenticity there appears to be a contradiction that needs sorting out. On the one hand, it has been argued that to be authentic a person must realize his being-in-situation by throwing himself wholeheartedly into his situation. On the other hand, it has been argued that authenticity involves refusing to live according to the expectations of others.

Recall Sartre's example of the former boring bourgeois turned soldier who is visited at the front by his wife. Sartre argues that the man cannot conform to his wife's former image of him without falling into inauthenticity. But how can a person throw himself into certain situations without conforming to the expectations of others? Conforming to the expectations of others is precisely what a committed response to certain situations requires. If the man is to throw himself wholeheartedly into his present situation – not the war but his meeting with his beloved wife – he must indulge her and make an effort to live up to her expectations of him in order to comfort her and preserve his relationship with her. It could be argued that behaving like this would be patronizing, but if patronizing someone involves treating them in a condescending manner then the man would patronize his wife far more if, having experienced horrors unknown to her, he confronted her in a superior, sullen and harsh manner.

Suppose the man refuses to indulge his wife and says to her, 'This war has put me in touch with the real me and I can no longer behave the way I used to.' A reasonable response to this remark would be that if the war really has put him in touch with himself then he ought to realize that he is free to adapt his behaviour to the requirements of any situation. To drive away a wife that he still loves because he cannot allow himself to conform to a former image of himself is not the behaviour of an authentic hero, but the behaviour of an inflexible, self-destructive idiot. Authenticity, it has been suggested, is an heroic ideal. As the movies repeatedly show us, the archetypal hero is both a lover and a fighter and can love or fight according to the demands of the situation. Moreover, his capacity to love is not corrupted by his capacity to fight, hate and face horrors, anymore than his capacity to fight is weakened by his capacity to love.

After World War II showed them how interdependent people are, Sartre and de Beauvoir began to acknowledge that authenticity involves conforming to some extent to the expectations of others. Their postwar writings acknowledge that a degree of social conformity is required for a person to meet the demands of most situations because most situations are human social situations to some extent.

People, they argue, are responsible for living up to the expectations that result from their social and historical circumstances. A person who seeks to evade this responsibility by refusing to be a person of his time acts in bad faith. He acts as though he is a fixed and self-sufficient island existing outside of society, politics and history, when in truth he is a person rooted in the social and political situation of his day and age who exists only in relation to his day and age. It is an existential truth of the human condition that, as John Donne said, 'No man is an island, entire of itself; every man is a piece of the continent, a part of the main' (*Meditation XVII*). It is therefore authentic for a person to acknowledge this; to acknowledge the existence and freedom of other people and the inevitability of having to have relations and dealings with them.

Nietzsche on authenticity – regret nothing

It's time now, as promised, to look at what Nietzsche has to say about authenticity. Like Sartre, he has a lot to say, and a fair amount of it quite similar to Sartre. Well, it's hardly surprising that great existentialist philosophers should think alike, especially as Nietzsche had a huge influence on all the twentieth-century existentialists. Nietzsche is one of those towering figures of philosophy who influenced and continues to influence just about everyone, from D. H. Lawrence to Lawrence of Arabia, from ghettoized Jews to Nazis, from Freudian psychoanalysts (including Freud himself) to the more intelligent type of German Bundesliga soccer manager. This is partly because his writings appear to offer something for everyone. The main reason, however, is that he is a profound and inspiring thinker who gets much further down into the complexities and peculiarities of life than the average, unimaginative, logic-chopping academic. Actually, 'logic-chopper' is one of Nietzsche's own terms of abuse. Nietzsche was very fond of wittily insulting other thinkers in his writings. Another reason why he is so popular with all the thinkers he didn't get around to insulting.

Bad faith, Sartre tells us, is a choice not to choose. It is *negative freedom*, freedom that denies, checks and represses itself. To exercise freedom negatively is to adopt what Nietzsche calls the *ascetic ideal*. The ascetic ideal values self-repression and self-denial above all else and for their own sake. A person who adopts the ascetic ideal does not, for example, value celibacy for the sexual health and peace of mind it brings, but only for the self-denial it involves. Opposite to the ascetic ideal is Nietzsche's notion of the *noble ideal*. The noble ideal involves the positive affirmation of freedom. A noble person positively affirms himself as a free being. He does not deny and repress his freedom but enjoys it and is constantly aware of it. He does this by acting decisively, overcoming difficulties, taking responsibility, refusing to regret and, most importantly, by choosing his own values. For Nietzsche, positive freedom is expansive, sometimes even reckless and violent. It triumphs in its own strength as a positive *will to power*.

Will to power, a key idea in Nietzsche's philosophy, can be either positive or negative. Positive will to power is power as it is commonly understood: power that is expansive, even explosive. Its opposite, however, is still will to power. A being that refuses to expand still has will to power. Soldiers making an orderly retreat refuse expansion but this does not mean they have lost their will to power. Likewise, a person who conserves his strength behind a barricade exercises will to power in inviting his enemy to spend his strength attacking that barricade. For Nietzsche, a person cannot not be a will to power, just as, according to Sartre, a person cannot not be free. Whereas Nietzsche has the concepts of positive and negative will to power, Sartre has the concepts of the positive freedom of the responsible, authentic person and the negative freedom of the inauthentic person who acts in bad faith choosing not to choose.

Sartre argues that freedom can value itself as the source of all values. This positive freedom involves the same principles as Nietzsche's noble ideal. It is a positive will to power. A person does not achieve a radical conversion to authenticity by rejecting and divorcing his former self through the exercise of bad faith, but by overcoming his former self, his former values, to become the creator of his own values.

Sartre's idea of a radical conversion to authenticity involves a person becoming something like Nietzsche's *Ubermensch*. If you've come across this German term before it might well evoke images of blond-haired, blue-eyed, jack-booted Nazi Stormtroopers goose-stepping in tight formation through the Brandenburg Gate, but it literally means 'overman'; the man who has overcome himself. As the creator of his own values the overman creates himself; he is the artist or author of his own life. In an article he wrote called 'Nietzsche on Authenticity' the Jewish philosopher Jacob Golomb (that's Golomb not Golum) says: 'The will to power is of a piece with the quest for authenticity – the will to become a free author (within the necessary limits) of one's own self. The optimal will to power is expressed by the ideally authentic Ubermensch' ('Nietzsche on Authenticity', p. 254).

Whatever a negative person or a person in bad faith identifies as a bad experience to be forgotten or denied, the artist or author of his own life, whose aim is to positively affirm his entire life, identifies as a learning experience that helped to make him stronger and wiser. He regrets nothing because every experience has contributed to making him what he is. In Nietzsche's view, he will not even regret his evil qualities, or what other people label his evil qualities. As the source of his own values he re-evaluates his evil qualities as his best qualities. His ability to do this is a true mark of his authenticity. 'The great epochs of our life are the occasions when we gain the courage to rebaptise our evil qualities as our best qualities' (*Beyond Good and Evil*, 116, p. 97).

In *Crime and Punishment*, a brilliant novel by the Russian existentialist writer Fyodor Dostoevsky, the central character Raskolnikov, in an attempt to escape his poverty, kills a mean old pawn-broker and her sister with an axe. It would have been far less drastic for Raskolnikov simply to claim welfare payments but there wasn't much of a social security system in St Petersburg in the 1860s. After committing double-murder, Raskolnikov tells himself he must strive to be like Napoleon, a man who has the strength of character to justify his crimes to himself. Unfortunately, unlike Napoleon, Raskolnikov lacks the audacity to shoulder his dirty deed and genuinely not care about it. In Nietzsche's words, he lacks the courage to 'redeem the past and to transform every "it was" into "thus I willed it"' (*Thus Spoke Zarathustra*, p. 161).

As Raskolnikov's ego is not sufficient to swallow the enormity of his crime, his only means of escaping his guilt is to lapse into an attitude of bad faith whereby he disowns himself by disowning his past. I am not saying that to be authentic you must go around killing mean old ladies with an axe without giving a damn about it, but rather that to be authentic you must take responsibility for all your actions whatever they are rather than try to disown them through bad faith and confession and the belief that you have been 'born again'.

To disown the past in bad faith and to redefine the past by assuming responsibility for it are radically different responses. If the aspiring convert to authenticity is to overcome bad faith he must take responsibility for the whole of his past without regret. A person who regrets wishes his past were different, he wishes he were not the free being he is and has been. A person who regrets fails to affirm the whole of his freedom and hence the whole of his life as the creation of his freedom. Nietzsche holds that the highest affirmation of life is the desire for eternal recurrence. For a person to truly affirm his freedom and his life as the creation of his freedom he must embrace the possibility of living it all over again in every detail an infinite number of times. Nietzsche writes beautifully so it is worth quoting his most famous passage on eternal recurrence in full:

> *The greatest weight.* – What, if some day or night a demon were to steal after you into your loneliest loneliness and say to you: 'This life as you now live it and have lived it, you will have to live once more and innumerable times more; and there will be nothing new in it, but every pain and every joy and every thought and every sigh and everything unutterably small or great in your life will have to return to you, all in the same succession and sequence

– even this spider and this moonlight between the trees, and even this moment and I myself. The eternal hourglass of existence is turned upside down again and again, and you with it, speck of dust!' Would you not throw yourself down and gnash your teeth and curse the demon who spoke thus? Or have you once experienced a tremendous moment when you would have answered him: 'You are a god and never have I heard anything more divine.' If this thought gained possession of you, it would change you as you are or perhaps crush you. The question in each and everything, 'Do you desire this once more and innumerable times more?' would lie upon your actions as the greatest weight. Or how well disposed would you have to become towards yourself and to life to crave nothing more fervently than this ultimate confirmation and seal. (*The Gay Science*, 341, pp. 273–274)

Nietzsche's uncompromising thought is that if you don't want to live your life over again then you're not living it right! He is asking you, 'Why are you doing that job now if you wouldn't want to do it again in your next life?' From a metaphysical point of view eternal recurrence is problematic: If eternal recurrence is true this life must be identical to the infinity of lives you have lived and will live, you can't change anything, and if you can't change anything you can't be free. That Nietzsche actually believes we live our lives over again an infinite number of times is debatable. Arguably, what matters to him is not whether or not eternal recurrence is the case but the moral acid test that the very idea of it provides.

Nietzsche's answer to the perennial moral question, 'How should I live?', is: Aspire to live in such a way that you want each and every moment of your life to recur eternally. Nietzsche calls this his *formula for greatness*. 'My formula for greatness for a human being is *amor fati* [love fate]: that one wants nothing to be other than it is, not in the future, not in the past, not in all eternity' (*Ecce Homo: How One Becomes What One Is*, p. 68). In rejecting and discarding his past like an old pair of boots, Raskolnikov fails to adopt Nietzsche's formula for greatness. It almost goes without saying that to become a true existentialist, to achieve authentic existence, you have to embrace Nietzsche's formula for greatness. A tough call, but that's how it is, maybe forever.

Heidegger on authenticity – authentic being-towards-death

Another existentialist philosopher who has a lot to say about authenticity, even if he failed miserably to be authentic thanks to his right-wing political leanings, is Heidegger. Heidegger holds that the project of authenticity involves a person affirming the inescapable truths of the human condition. In this he is very much like Sartre, which is not surprising seeing as – politics aside – he was Sartre's second biggest influence. Sartre's biggest influence, by the way, was Husserl who was Heidegger's teacher but not Sartre's, although Sartre did study Husserl in depth on a nine-month sabbatical at the French Institute in Berlin in 1933. Connections, connections.

Anyway, as we've seen, Sartre's account of authenticity emphasizes assuming and affirming freedom. Heidegger's account of authenticity, on the other hand, emphasizes assuming and affirming mortality. Authenticity for Heidegger is principally *authentic being-towards-death*. This all sounds rather morbid, and indeed it is morbid in the dictionary sense of 'having an unusual interest in death', but what Heidegger recognizes is that people can have an authentic or an inauthentic attitude towards the fact that they are going to die. Heidegger refers to the being of each human being as *Dasein*, German for 'being-there'. Dasein refers to a person's unique spatial and temporal situatedness in the world. Heidegger says, 'Death is Dasein's *ownmost* possibility' (*Being and Time*, p. 307).

The constant possibility of death in the present, the inevitability of death in the future, is central to the very being of Dasein. A person's present is what it is by virtue of its finitude, a finitude arising from the promise of death that perpetually haunts the present. Authentic being-towards-death involves a person fully acknowledging in the way he lives his life that his time is finite and his death inevitable. By recognizing that he himself must die, rather than merely recognizing that people die, a person ceases to view himself in bad faith as simply another Other and realizes that he exists as the wholly unique possibility of his own death. Heidegger says, 'The non-relational character of death, as understood in anticipation, individualises Dasein down to itself' (*Being and Time*, p. 30).

Not surprisingly, people tend to acquire an authentic 'I must die' attitude as they grow older. Becoming aware of one's own mortality is a key part of growing up and becoming a genuine adult. Young people, on the other hand, tend to have an inauthentic 'other people die' attitude. The older and younger generations are perhaps divided more by their attitude to mortality than by the fact that the former like tweed and tranquillity while the latter like hoodies and rap. Young people, at least in Western societies, tend to view elderly people as a totally separate group from the rest of humankind, as rather repulsive creatures who were always old and decaying and near death, rather than as people who were once young who have just happened to survive long enough to become old and near death. The dismissiveness and contempt that is often shown by the young towards the old both reinforces this separating off of elderly people and is a symptom of it.

A youth once mocked a man for reaching seventy. 'Don't knock me' the older man replied. 'I'm sure you hope to live as long as I have yourself.' Of course, some young adults say things like, 'I'm going to kill myself before I get old; better to burn out than fade away!' They don't really mean it, anymore than young children know what they are talking about when they say, 'I'm not going to die, I'm going to live forever.' Due to their limited experience of life the young are full of crap, they can't help it, or as *The Bible* more eloquently puts it, 'When I was a child, I spake as a child, I understood as a child, I thought as a child: but when I became a man, I put away childish things' (*1 Corinthians 13*).

Young people tend to view themselves as a distinct group also, as immortals who will always be young, rather than as people who will inevitably become old and near death if they survive long enough. No doubt this attitude is part of the arrogance of youth and the young can be excused it on the grounds that they are immature and naïve. Not to think they will grow old and die is the privilege of youth and doubtless the old and enlightened envy them this privilege. Nonetheless, their attitude is in bad faith because it involves viewing both youth and old age as fixed states rather than as phases of the same relentless process.

It is even bad faith for young people to think of old people as nearer death than they are. Ok, so nobody lives much beyond one hundred even these days, so elderly people are nearer death in one sense, but death – that proverbial bus that might knock you down tomorrow – is an ever present possibility for people of any age. The seventy year old might well outlive the youth who mocks him for being seventy, especially if the youth rides a motorcycle. Sartre describes death as an elastic limit that can be nearer or further away depending on circumstances. If a person was in a high fever yesterday, he was closer to death yesterday than he is today now that he has recovered.

Only by realizing that he is the wholly unique possibility of his own death does a person cease to treat himself as though he is a copy of the next man and of all men. For Heidegger, this is the real meaning of authenticity. The authentic person, like the authentic artefact, is the genuine, bona fide article, not a reproduction or a replica. Though his life may resemble the lives of many others, he is, nonetheless, his own person and he identifies himself as his own person.

It is only when a person fully realizes that he must die and acts in accordance with this realization that he truly begins to exist and live in his own right. In taking responsibility for his own death he takes responsibility for his own life and the way he chooses to live it. To truly realize and affirm mortality is to overcome bad faith. This view fits in neatly with the claim that authenticity involves living without regret. If the affirmation of freedom demands that a person affirm his *entire* life without regret, then it follows that he must also affirm his mortality. This affirmation does not involve relishing the prospect of death – it is not a suicidal death wish – but it does involve a person acknowledging that his life is finite and the implications this has for the way he lives his life.

A key characteristic of Nietzsche's overman is his recognition and acceptance of his own mortality. The overman is a person who, though fully aware of his mortality, is not petrified with fear at the thought of it. He does not allow his fear of death to prevent him from taking certain risks and living his life to the full. Simone de Beauvoir argues that this attitude towards death is an essential characteristic of the adventurous person who values the affirmation of his freedom above timid self-preservation. 'Even his death is not an evil since he is a man only in so far as he is mortal: he must assume it as the natural limit of his life, as the risk implied by every step' (*The Ethics of Ambiguity*, p. 82). Unadventurous people who fail to live life to the full because they fear death, still die. They die, however, never having really lived; having already died, metaphorically, many times. This is what Shakespeare meant when he wrote, 'Cowards die many times before their deaths; The valiant never taste of death but once' (*Julius Caesar*, II, ii).

Outwardly, the life of the person who has embraced his mortality may be no different from that of his neighbour who has not, but in embracing his mortality he has made his life uniquely his own, he has achieved authenticity, at least in the Heideggerian sense of authentic being-towards-death. A true existentialist should never live as though he has forever, frittering away his time and putting off indefinitely the things he really wants to do. I'm not going to add, however, that he should live his life as though each day were his last, because a person can't achieve much in life if he doesn't make relatively long-term plans and wait a while for the best time to act.

I once knew a guy who always tried to live for the moment, immediately taking every pleasure and indulgence he could get his hands on. He worshipped at the shrine of instant gratification and held all

patience, prudence and moderation in contempt as deferred gratification. He regularly used the phrase 'deferred gratification' when derid-
ing people who limited their drinking, saved their money or retired
early. He adhered admirably to his philosophy and had some wild times
but he became an alcoholic before the age of thirty and met his death
by misadventure.

If a person really did live each day as though it were his last he
would spend each day panicking while partying and rapidly reduce
himself to a nervous, drunken, insolvent wreck. Nonetheless, a person
should live his life recognizing that each moment, each day, is precious
and utterly irreplaceable. Quitting smoking, eating bran, belting-up in
the car and avoiding assassination will probably buy you more time but
that's not the point. Although it is sensible to do what you can to pro-
long life, there is no point in buying yourself more time if you don't
make the most of it. As Abraham Lincoln, a great man who certainly
made the most of his 56 years, 1 month and 24 days is supposed to
have said but apparently didn't, 'In the end, it's not the years in your life
that count. It's the life in your years.'

Be a true existentialist, be authentic, seize your freedom, seize the
day. *Carpe diem* as the noble Romans used to say.

5 Existential Counselling

Earlier, I mentioned existential counselling, a lucrative practice in which good listeners with a knowledge of existentialism presume to help other people start living more honest, positive, regret-free lives. As this book is kind of an exercise in existential counselling, if only because it offers counsel on how to be an existentialist, I thought that by way of conclusion I'd return to the subject of existential counselling and say some more about it. After all, you may feel you need counselling after reading this book, or you may be thinking of getting yourself a big beard (ladies included), a wise expression, a brass plate and a leather couch and setting yourself up as an existential counsellor.

The broad aim of existential counselling is to help people make changes in their lives or in themselves that are for the better. The counsellor will encourage the client (as the patient / customer is called) to explore what he understands by 'making changes for the better'. During the counselling process the client's ideas concerning what is better for him or her may well change. In emphasizing that there is nothing fixed that we are, that we are free at least to strive to overcome our present attitudes, habits, failings and hang-ups, the existential counsellor will encourage the client to recognize that the broad aim of self-improvement is achievable. If we are what we are then there is no hope of deliberately changing what we are, we are stuck with what we are, but if we are a product of our choices then there is always hope of overcoming and altering the way we are now.

One of the main tasks of the existential counsellor is to convince the client that he or she is free in the way described, and, as such, has a capacity for self-improvement. The process will involve something like philosophical debate, pitched at whatever level the client can cope with, but must not involve bullying the client into confronting hard existential truths before he or she is ready to confront them.

Here is the big difference between this book and existential counselling. This book just lays the hard existential truths on the line with little or no soft soap or bubble bath. A good existential counsellor, however, like a good lover, is slow and gentle. As Emmy Van Deurzen-Smith says in her book, *Existential Counselling and Psychotherapy in Practice*, 'Basic counselling skills such as an ability to listen rather than guess, to reflect rather than distort the client's meaning and to reassure rather than confuse the client are assumed' (*Existential Counselling and Psychotherapy in Practice*, p. 236). It is, of course, always in a counsellor's *financial* interest to be slow and gentle, to help his or her clients at the pace of an over-paid slug on tranquillizers.

Existential counselling places huge emphasis on delving into the client's past, on piecing together the client's unique biography. Sartre illustrated the method of existential psychoanalysis that lies behind existential counselling by writing several extremely detailed psychoanalytical biographies of famous French writers. Apart from probing into the lurid psychological depths of Charles Baudelaire, Jean Genet and Gustave Flaubert, these biographies *show* how existential psychoanalysis ought to be conducted. Just like Sartre with his French writers, existential counsellors make every effort to preserve the individual rather than pigeonhole him and explain him away by applying a bunch of universal psychological labels to a description of his unique personality. The aim is not to say this person is depressed or neurotic or whatever, but to discover his unique *fundamental choice* of himself.

A person's choices can be traced back to a fundamental or original choice of himself made in response to a particular childhood event that occurred at the dawning of his self-consciousness. The event may have been trivial in itself – a fight with his sister over the last tea cake, for example – but his response to it is hugely significant in that it is the start of a process in which he chooses actions that affirm or deny his view of himself as a certain type of person. The actions that a person chooses in response to his fundamental choice comprise his *fundamental project*. A person's fundamental choice is arbitrary and groundless but it is nonetheless a choice of self that establishes grounds for all subsequent choosing. It is worth repeating that each person's fundamental choice is unique and can only be discovered through a detailed exploration of their personal history.

Sartre, Laing and other existential psychoanalysts hold that it is possible for a person to undergo a *radical conversion* in which he redefines himself, hopefully for the better, by establishing a new fundamental choice of himself. Each person's capacity to have a radical conversion is of the utmost importance as far as the process of existential counselling is concerned. Question: How many existential counsellors does it take to change a light bulb? Answer: One, but both the counsellor and the light bulb must believe change is possible.

According to Sartre, Gustave Flaubert, the author of *Madame Bovary*, had a radical conversion in his early twenties that totally changed the direction of his life. It wasn't brought on by an existential counsellor, however, but by events in Flaubert's life reaching a crisis point. To understand Flaubert's radical conversion you need to know a bit about his family background. In fact, Sartre thinks you need to know absolutely everything about Flaubert's family background to understand his radical conversion, which is why Sartre wrote just about the longest book ever written dissecting every minuscule detail of Flaubert's life, times and potty training. In order to keep this book mercifully short, however, we will have to make do with a potted version of Flaubert's family history.

If, like me, you often find yourself saying, 'I blame the parents,' even before you know the details of the sad case that is the damaged youth confronting you, then hearing Flaubert's story can only reinforce your confidence in that particular well-worn prejudice. By screwing their child up, however, unlike most crap parents, Flaubert's parents inadvertently helped him become one of the greatest figures in the history of literature.

Gustave's granny died giving birth to his mum, Caroline. His granddad was heartbroken. The guilt Caroline felt over killing her mum was reinforced by the death of her dad when she was ten. The dad had not loved his daughter enough to want to go on living. Caroline resurrected her dad and so eased her guilt by marrying his double, Achille-Cléophas Flaubert, a stiff, domineering, successful doctor several years her senior. At first the marriage was happy. Caroline doted on her husband and a son, Achille, was born. By the time Gustave arrived, however, Caroline had lost a number of children and her husband was having affairs with various mistresses.

Caroline wanted a daughter, a female companion to compensate for her lonely childhood, so Gustave was a disappointment. Not only that, but as the two siblings who immediately preceded him had died, baby Gustave was not expected to live. There was little affection in the skilful care that the disappointing, futureless infant received; it aimed only at pacifying him. Sartre identifies Flaubert's passivity as his fundamental choice of himself, at least until he underwent his radical conversion. He was not encouraged to respond, to feel that he had a purpose, to feel that he could be something more than an object his mum was obliged to powder and pamper.

Gustave fared no better with his dad, whose attentions and hopes were directed towards Gustave's older brother, Achille, who eventually became a successful doctor like his dad. Gustave was deeply jealous of smart arsed Achille. Pacified, overlooked as a person, Gustave's intellectual development was painfully slow. He was unable to read at the age of seven. His family further reinforced the low self-esteem at the heart of his listlessness by viewing him as an idiot – hence the ironic title of Sartre's vast book, *The Family Idiot*.

Gustave was eventually taught to read by the local priest. Though still passive in his general demeanour and given to meditative stupors that made him appear a simpleton, Gustave grasped his new ability and by the age of nine he was writing stories. Without asking Gustave what he thought about it, Achille-Cléophas decided his son would become a lawyer. Passive as ever, Gustave followed his dad's plan, all the while developing a psychosomatic nervous disorder.

The defining moment of Gustave's life occurred in 1844 when he suffered a nervous breakdown, possibly an epileptic fit. Incapacitated by this breakdown he was unable to pursue the career his dad had chosen for him. His crisis, possibly self-induced, was the opportunity for Gustave to finally free himself from his dad's domination and become a writer. The invalid, being no good for anything better, was left to write. The idiot was at last free to transform himself into a genius.

For Sartre, Flaubert's crisis was a radical conversion to authenticity, an act of self-assertion in which he finally dispensed with his passivity, his choice not to choose, his bad faith. Through an act that had the outward appearance of a mental collapse, but was in fact a positive affirmation of freedom, he ceased to exist primarily for others and began to exist for himself.

In making the client aware of his inalienable freedom, in helping him to discover that, like Flaubert, like everyone, he is not a fixed entity but the product of a fundamental choice that can be changed, the existential counsellor aims to inspire the client to begin formulating strategies of overcoming and empowerment. At this point the counsellor can advise the client on possible patterns of behaviour that he might adopt in order to bring about positive changes in his relationship with himself, the world and other people.

The existential counsellor, Viktor Frankl, gives us the example of a man who had a fear of sweating in the presence of others that caused him to sweat. Frankl encouraged him to choose an attitude of *pride* towards his capacity to sweat. To say to himself when he met people who triggered his anxiety, 'I only sweated a litre before, but now I'm going to pour out at least ten litres!' According to Frankl, this strategy very quickly allowed the man to free himself of his phobia.

In many cases, a client may not need the counsellor's advice to develop strategies. Strategies will occur to the client as a result of realizing he is free, that radical change is possible and so on. The very fact that the client is formulating his own strategies shows he is making progress. Existential counselling always encourages clients to take the initiative. This is not surprising given that the main object of the existential counselling exercise is personal empowerment.

Achieving an intellectual awareness of his own freedom might, for example, be a client's first step towards conquering his arachnophobia. (Former American President George W. Bush and former British Prime Minister Tony Blair now suffer from Iraqnophobia for which there is no cure.) Realizing he is not stuck with being a person who fears spiders, the client will realize that he must, in a certain sense, be choosing himself as a person who has no choice but to fear spiders. He reaffirms this choice every time he acts fearfully towards spiders by killing them. The solution to his phobia is to refrain by an act of will – which, admittedly, will be difficult at first – from all behaviour that confirms his false belief that his fear is something he is stuck with. By abandoning this self-perpetuating project of irrational fear he should eventually realize that there is, in fact, nothing to fear from common house spiders. If he lives in Australia, however, where there are various poisonous spiders including the deadly black widow, he might be better to preserve his arachnophobia. Phobias and neuroses are not always bad, they can protect us and incline us in useful directions.

To the same degree that the existential counsellor aims to put the client in touch with his or her freedom and capacity to change, he also seeks to reconcile him or her to certain basic facts of the human condition as identified by existentialism. For example, it follows from the fact that we are always in constant process of becoming that we will never be completely fulfilled – not even if we win the lottery, swim with dolphins and drive a tank over a bus. There will always be something more we want, something we feel is missing, because to hanker after something, to believe the grass is greener on the other side, is fundamental to a creature that lacks itself in the present and continually strives to be at one with itself in the future. Existential counselling works with the assumption that people would spare themselves a great deal of further misery if they only realized this fact instead of thinking that there is something seriously wrong with them because they don't feel extremely happy and satisfied all of the time.

In one sense, existential counselling aims to show people that they do not have to put up with what they are. In another sense, it aims to show them that the very fact of being alive presents us all with certain unavoidable difficulties. Consider the attitude of existential counselling to anxiety, as expressed by Gary S. Belkin in his book, *Introduction to Counselling*. We have already seen that, according to the existentialists, anxiety or angst is an inescapable feature of realizing we are free. Belkin writes: 'The existential counsellor, unlike the psychoanalytic or behavioural counsellor, does not view anxiety as a dangerous or neurotic condition. Rather, anxiety is seen as a fundamental condition of existence. The job of the counsellor is to help the client accept anxiety as part of his or her fundamental being' (*Introduction to Counselling*, p. 187). Accepting a degree of anxiety might well save a person from an upward spiral of anxiety where he gets anxious about being anxious.

The ultimate aim of existential counselling is to help clients discover meaning in their lives. On the face of it, this seems a strange aim for a form of counselling that is backed by a philosophy claiming life to be essentially absurd and meaningless. But what must be understood is what follows from this belief in the essential meaninglessness of life. Namely, that only people themselves can give their lives any meaning through the goals they set themselves, the choices they make and the actions they take. Existential counselling has the optimistic goal of seeking to show the client that his or her life is an unwritten book that only he or she can write.

Life has only the meaning you choose to give it.

Bibliography

Allen, Woody, *Side Effects* (New York: Ballantine, 1991).

Belkin, Gary S., *Introduction to Counselling* (Dubuque, IA: W. C. Brown, 1988).

Camus, Albert, *The Myth of Sisyphus,* trans. Justin O'Brien (London: Penguin, 2006).

Cox, Gary, *The Sartre Dictionary* (London and New York: Continuum, 2008).

de Beauvoir, Simone, *The Ethics of Ambiguity*, trans. Bernard Frechtman (New York: Citadel Press, 2000).

Dickens, Charles, *Bleak House* (London: Penguin, 2003).

Donne, John, *Meditation XVII*, in Donne, *Selected Poems* (London: Penguin, 2006).

Dostoevsky, Fyodor, *Crime and Punishment*, trans. David Magarshack (London: Penguin, 2007).

Flaubert, Gustave, *Madame Bovary*, trans. Geoffrey Wall (London: Penguin, 2003).

Golomb, Jacob, 'Nietzsche on Authenticity', *Philosophy Today*, vol. 34, 1990.

Heidegger, Martin, *Being and Time,* trans. John Macquarrie and Edward Robinson (Oxford: Blackwell, 1993).

Kierkegaard, Søren, *Concluding Unscientific Postscript,* trans. Alastair Hannay (Cambridge: Cambridge University Press, 2009).

Laing, Ronald D., *The Divided Self: An Existential Study in Sanity and Madness* (London: Penguin, 1990).

McCulloch, Gregory, *Using Sartre: An Analytical Introduction to Early Sartrean Themes* (London and New York: Routledge, 1994).

Merleau-Ponty, Maurice, *Phenomenology of Perception*, trans. Colin Smith (London and New York: Routledge, 2002).

Murdoch, Iris, *Sartre: Romantic Rationalist* (London: Fontana, 1968).

Nietzsche, Friedrich, *Beyond Good and Evil: Prelude to a Philosophy of the Future*, trans. R. J. Hollingdale (London: Penguin, 2003).

—, *Ecce Homo: How One Becomes What One Is*, trans. R. J. Hollingdale (London: Penguin, 2004).

—, *The Gay Science*, trans. Walter Kaufmann (New York: Vintage Press, 1974).

—, *Thus Spoke Zarathustra*, trans. Graham Parkes (Oxford: Oxford University Press, 2005).

Plato, *The Republic*, trans. Desmond Lee (London: Penguin, 2003).

Sartre, Jean-Paul, *The Age of Reason*, trans. David Caute (London: Penguin, 2001). See also *Roads to Freedom*.

—, *Being and Nothingness*: *An Essay on Phenomenological Ontology*, trans. Hazel E. Barnes (London and New York: Routledge, 2003).

—, *The Childhood of a Leader*, in Sartre, *The Wall*, trans. Lloyd Alexander (New York: New Directions, 1988).

—, *Existentialism and Humanism*, trans. Philip Mairet (London: Methuen, 1993).

—, *The Family Idiot* vols. 1–5, trans. Carol Cosman (Chicago: University of Chicago Press, 1981).

—, *In Camera* (*No Exit* or *Behind Closed Doors*), trans. Stuart Gilbert, in *In Camera and Other Plays* (Harmondsworth: Penguin, 1990).

—, *Nausea*, trans. Robert Baldick (London: Penguin, 2000).

—, *Roads to Freedom*. A trilogy of novels, including: *The Age of Reason*, *The Reprieve* and *Iron in the Soul* (London: Penguin, 2001, 2005 & 2004 respectively).

—, *The Transcendence of the Ego, A Sketch for a Phenomenological Description*, trans. Andrew Brown (London and New York: Routledge, 2004).

—, *Truth and Existence*, trans. Adrian van den Hoven (Chicago: University of Chicago Press, 1995).

—, *War Diaries: Notebooks from a Phoney War, 1939–1940*, trans. Quintin Hoare (London: Verso, 2000).

van Deurzen-Smith, Emmy, *Existential Counselling and Psychotherapy in Practice* (Thousand Oaks, CA: Sage, 2002).

Further Reading

Blackham, Harold John, *Six Existentialist Thinkers* (London and New York: Routledge, 1991).

Camus, Albert, *The Outsider* (*The Stranger*), trans. Joseph Laredo (London: Penguin, 2000).

Cox, Gary, *Sartre: A Guide for the Perplexed* (London and New York: Continuum, 2006).

—, *Sartre and Fiction* (London and New York: Continuum, 2009).

Detmer, David, *Freedom as a Value: A Critique of the Ethical Theory of Jean-Paul Sartre* (La Salle, IL: Open Court, 1986).

Earnshaw, Stephen, *Existentialism: A Guide for the Perplexed* (London and New York: Continuum, 2006).

Frankl, Viktor E., *Man's Search for Meaning* (London: Rider, 2004).

Laycock, Stephen, *Nothingness and Emptiness: A Buddhist Engagement with the Ontology of Jean-Paul Sartre* (Albany, NY: SUNY Press, 2001).

Loy, David, *Lack and Transcendence: The Problem of Death and Life in Psychotherapy, Existentialism and Buddhism* (New York: Prometheus, 2003).

Panza, Christopher and Gale, Gregory, *Existentialism for Dummies* (Oxford: Wiley-Blackwell, 2008).

Vatican Index of Prohibited Books (*Index Librorum Prohibitorum*) and the works prohibited therein. Works by Bacon, Galileo, Descartes, Milton, Pascal, Locke, Voltaire, Hume, Rousseau, Flaubert, Zola, Sartre, etc.

Warnock, Mary, *Existentialism* (Oxford: Oxford University Press, 1992).

Index